The Place
We Call Home

A VOICE FROM THE MONASTERY

The Place We Call Home

Spiritual Pilgrimage as a Path to God

Murray Bodo, O.F.M.

PARACLETE PRESS
Brewster, Massachusetts

Scripture quotations are taken from the New Revised Standard Version of the Bible, copyright 1989, Division of Christian Education of the National Council of the Churches of Christ in the United States of America. Used by permission. All rights reserved.

Library of Congress Cataloging–in–Publication Data

Bodo, Murry.
   The place we call home : spiritual pilgrimage as a path to God /
   Murry Bodo
        p.   cm.—(A voice from the monastery)
   ISBN 1–55725–357–9
   1. Christian life—Catholic authors. 2. Bodo, Murry. I. Title.
  II. Series.
   BX2350.3 .B64 2004
   263' .041—dc22

                                        2003025960

10 9 8 7 6 5 4 3 2 1

ISBN 1-55725-357-9

Published by Paraclete Press
Brewster, Massachusetts
www.paracletepress.com

Printed in the United States of America.

For Susan Saint Sing and Herbert Lomas,
so much a part of my pilgrimage

Contents

PART ONE

The Pilgrim's Map

Mainly it's the stories we carry with us,
the tales of those who've gone before,
those who've made their own map,
as we will make ours.

The stories and rituals passed down
from generation to generation.
They will help us make our map.

The stories, rituals, the Spirit of God.
Of these shall we be created anew.

Of these three is pilgrimage: story, ritual, Spirit.
How we listen and do and pray
becomes the map we make.

✳ *Setting Forth*

The bus rumbled and loomed above me like an ocean
liner as it idled beside the small Greyhound bus depot
next to the *Elite Laundry* where Mother worked. With
door open and the driver standing beside it checking
tickets, the bus seemed to me then like Alice's "Looking
Glass," which, once I passed through it, would open a
whole new world to me—a world so fantastic and
removed from Gallup, New Mexico, that I would be
transformed into one of the saints or heroes of the books
that brought me to this moment of departure.

It was the end of August, 1951. I was fourteen years
old—a boy about to leave home for a Franciscan seminary
1500 miles away in Cincinnati, Ohio. An only child, I
stood by my mother and father who were helpless to
deter me from what must have seemed to them a pre-
mature, foolhardy decision to leave home and begin my
studies for the Franciscan priesthood.

Pius XII was Pope and had been since the year after I
was born. Eisenhower was President of the United States. It
was the height of the Cold War, and Senator Joe McCarthy
was beginning to ferret out the Communists and their
sympathizers that he saw hidden everywhere in America.

The world was different then—a different Church with a Latin liturgy (a Latin I was about to begin learning). Priests wore Roman collars and cassocks, and Sisters wore full religious habits. Catholic schools bulged with students taught largely by Sisters, Brothers, and priests. Seminaries, too, were filled to capacity with young men straight out of the eighth grade who had a future that looked to me full of adventure and travel, while striving for holiness and saving souls.

All I needed to do was climb aboard the Greyhound bus and begin a pilgrimage that would take me to Ohio where thirteen years of study, prayer and religious discipline would end in ordination to the priesthood. This trip promised to be both a geographical and a temporal journey consisting of four years of high school seminary, followed by a year-long novitiate, after which I would profess temporary vows of poverty, chastity, and obedience as a Franciscan Friar. After the third year of college seminary, I would profess solemn vows for life, and then five years later be ordained a Franciscan priest. I hoped then, to return to the Southwest as a Navajo missionary like the priests and Sisters who inspired me.

The bus continued to rumble—idling; my mother and father and I waited. Pete, another seminarian-to-be, older than I, waited with his parents—till it was time. Then we kissed our mothers, shook hands with our fathers, and climbed the brief stairs into a life that would change us forever. The Church and the world, though we did not know it then, were also about to change in ways we never could have imagined. Pete, whose name is now Friar Diego, was ordained in 1960, and I was ordained in 1964, one year after the closing of the Second Vatican Council. I had studied Latin for thirteen years, read philosophy and theology in Latin, and my first Mass was partially in English. The vernacular languages were beginning to replace Latin as the liturgical language of the Catholic Church. Within a short time, priests would no longer face the altar with their backs to the people. The altar now resembled a table around which priest and people gathered for the Eucharistic meal.

These very simple gestures created seismic changes in the relationship between priest and lay people. The priest was now seen as one chosen from among the people to lead them in their communal Eucharistic celebration. No longer was he elevated above the rest, set apart, distanced by a sanctuary whose Communion rail was the boundary beyond which the people were not to enter. Priest and lay people together became more visibly a pilgrim church, traveling and worshiping together.

The world, too, had changed. President John F. Kennedy was assassinated the year before I was ordained, and America was in the midst of the Vietnam War. Far from abating the Cold War had become hot, at least in Southeast Asia. Things seemed to be falling apart, and the Church was changing the rituals and practices that the boy waiting to board the bus thought were immutable.

In fact, when I first stepped onto the Greyhound bus bound for Cincinnati, via Amarillo, St. Louis, and Indianapolis, I believed my own life and the life of the world was experiencing a spiritual rebirth signaled by the popularity of national figures like TV personality Bishop Fulton J. Sheen, the Trappist monk Thomas Merton, and social activists like Catholic Worker founder, Dorothy Day.

Nor was this simply adolescent naiveté. There was in the 1950's, in the Catholic Church, a tangible renaissance of spirituality and devotion, of practical concern and care for the poor. There was a uniformity of faith and practice articulated with grace and clarity in the pronouncements and encyclical letters of Pope Pius XII; in the "unchangeable" Latin liturgy, the exact rituals of the seven sacraments, para-liturgical devotions like the rosary, the way of the cross, the novena, and the rigid rules of fast and abstinence. We were all connected in faith and practice spelled out in the formulas of the Baltimore Catechism.

How consoling that was to me as an only child living in a border town between New Mexico and Arizona! The Church and its doctrines and practices gave me a sense of being connected to others, to a mystical body larger than my own small body—a community and communion of believers with Christ as its head and the Holy Spirit as its soul.

✳ ✳ ✳ ✳

The bus stopped in Cincinnati. What this journey began, however, did not end with ordination, but continued on into a sense that life itself is a pilgrimage. Forty years after the Second Vatican Council, the brave new world and the renewed Church that the Council envisioned, is again unraveling. The Cold War has been replaced by rampant terrorism and the threat of interreligious hatred erupting into a nuclear holocaust. The Catholic Church is racked with sexual scandal and cover-ups. New vocations to the priesthood and to religious life are minimal, and the laity still struggle to win their place in the Church, a place promised them by Vatican II. The pilgrimage continues, for we are all—people and institutions—on the pilgrim way.

When I look back now, after nearly fifty years, at the young boy riding the Greyhound bus from Gallup to Cincinnati, I see how individualistic my pilgrimage was then. *I* was going to the seminary; *I* was going to be a missionary, and saint. *I* was aware of and interested in Pete and other people on the bus, in my teachers and fellow seminarians, and later in my confreres in the novitiate and clericate, but it was only gradually, through a long period of humbling spiritual aridity, that the *I* lost its self-preoccupation and moved toward an *I-thou,* that led to a *we.*

I gradually began to see that all of us on the bus, *we,* were on the same journey. *We* were one body on that bus, and at the seminary, so that by the time of ordination, *we* had replaced *I* as my dominant vision; *we* were all on the same pilgrimage.

The Constitution on the Sacred Liturgy of the Second Vatican Council puts it better than I can.

> In the liturgy on earth *we* are given a foretaste and share of the liturgy of heaven, celebrated in the holy city of Jerusalem, the goal of *our* pilgrimage, where Christ is seated at the right hand of God, as minister of the sanctuary and of the true tabernacle.
>
> With the whole company of heaven *we* sing a hymn of praise to the Lord; as *we* reverence the memory of the saints, *we* hope to have some part with them, and to share in their *fellowship*; *we* wait for the Savior, *our* Lord Jesus Christ, until he, who is *our* life, appears, and *we* appear with him in glory. . . . (Italics mine)

The pilgrim way is communal, and in the shared journey the *I* finds its true identity. That is the work of pilgrimage, the transformation that is effected by and on the pilgrim way. That realization gives hope, no matter what is happening around *us.*

✳ *The Longing*

I reach down inside to that place to which I've been journeying my whole life, the place all the outer journeys have ultimately led to, and I try to understand the pilgrim heart in me and why it leads me ever away and back again.

I have always loved the pilgrim narratives of the Bible and of other literature. Exile and wandering, return and setting out again—the heart moving toward its final goal—the heart finding God within, who then sends one forth again. This is the dynamic, not only of the individual pilgrim heart, but of the people of God, all the people who live on this earth as sojourners longing for an eternal home.

Pilgrimages are not about one place being more holy than another, for God is everywhere. Making pilgrimages involves a response to something inside us that longs to move *toward*, that seeks the holy *beyond*.

Nor is this longing for something "out there" merely escapism; for what the pilgrim soon learns is that there is no mythical land of Oz "where troubles melt like lemon drops." If anything, the pilgrim way only focuses and intensifies our experience, which, when we were home, was diffused by distraction, responsibility, and busyness.

Unless we are persons of prayer and uncommon contemplation, our daily lives routinely detour deeper thoughts and a quiet looking at the world around us. But as soon as we set out on a journey, as I did as a young boy traveling east to the seminary, the world begins to unfold in a more enticing way, and we start to notice and anticipate that something grand might happen. Here is how the young boy Pip describes leaving home in Charles Dickens' coming-of-age novel, *Great Expectations.*

> I deliberated with an aching heart whether I would not get down when we changed horses and walk back, and have another evening at home, and a better parting. We changed, and I had not made up my mind, and still reflected for my comfort that it would be quite practicable to get down and walk back, when we changed again. . . .
>
> We changed again, and yet again, and it was now too late and too far to go back, and I went on.   And the mists had all solemnly risen now, and the world lay spread before me.

There's something almost breathless in Pip's last sentence, something we've all experienced at some time in our life. To go on a pilgrimage, or to perceive one's life as a pilgrimage, is more often than not at least partially motivated by everything implied in "the mists had all solemnly risen now, and the world lay spread before me." It is what one experiences in a deeply religious conversion.   Like the Apostle Paul, when the scales of blindness fall from his eyes, the convert begins to see the world in a whole new and exciting way. It is redeemed—shining with God's presence.

How many times have we as adults still asked ourselves one way or another, "I wonder what I'm going to be when I grow up?" The childhood question is still there, smoldering in our hearts, and it is possible that the embers will break into flame, lighting the way for a change in our lives. This is another dimension of pilgrimage: the possibility that I will somehow be changed and return renewed, alive again to my own world with its wonders and graces.

Sometimes, of course, the progress of that change is itself more intense and painful than what we thought we were fleeing from. Here, for example, is the beginning of Herman Melville's, *Moby Dick*.

> Call me Ishmael. . . . Whenever I find myself growing grim about the mouth; whenever it is a damp, drizzly November in my soul; whenever I find myself involuntarily pausing before coffin warehouses, and bringing up the rear of every funeral I meet; and especially whenever my hypos get such an upper hand of me, that it requires a strong moral principle to prevent me from deliberately stepping into the street, and methodically knocking people's hats off—then I account it high time to get to sea as soon as I can.

And so Ishmael goes to sea on a whaling ship, but there he encounters Captain Ahab and the white whale whom Captain Ahab's own dark heart and need for vengeance sees as evil and dark—something to be destroyed. And that is the irony of the book and of every pilgrimage: we bring with us on the journey who we are. We are quite capable of projecting our own evil on the world around us, instead of seeing the good that is there, and discerning good from evil both in the world and in our own hearts.

How powerful, then, for our own pilgrimages are Ishmael's words at the end of his dark journey aboard the whaling vessel, the *Pequod*.

The drama's done. Why then does anyone step forth?–
Because one did survive the wreck. . . . For almost one
whole day and night I floated on a soft and dirge-like
main. On the second day, a sail drew near, nearer, and
picked me up at last. It was the devious-cruising Rachel,
that in her retracing search after her missing children, only
found another orphan.

How poignantly anti-climactic! After the death of
Ahab roped to Moby Dick as he plunged into the sea;
and after the sinking of the ship and the drowning of the
crew, all Ishmael can say with Job is, "And I only am
escaped to tell thee," a quote from the book of Job that
Melville puts at the beginning of the Epilogue. This
makes the book a cautionary tale for any pilgrim who is
naive about the dangers and pitfalls of the quest.

❊ Beginnings of the Quest

As we respond to our longings to go on pilgrimage, we look for guidance, we look to those who have gone before us.

There's a small sixteenth-century engraving from the title page of *Information for Pilgrims Unto the Holy Land* that illustrates what it meant to be a pilgrim in the late Middle Ages. A pilgrim strides forth confidently, leaving behind a walled city with its brave parapets and towers from which flags flap in the wind.

Standing half-in and half-out of the city gate, another figure watches the pilgrim. This second figure typifies the one who wants to venture forth, but needs to keep one foot within the safety of the town, inside its protective walls. His right hand covers his heart as if to protect it and hold in the desire to follow in the pilgrim's footsteps. The pilgrim's eyes are fixed on the journey ahead; the other man's eyes are fixed on the pilgrim. Then, as now, the pilgrim is the one who dares to set forth; the stay-at-home hesitates on the threshold of his or her safe, familiar world.

In the Middle Ages safety and familiarity were important, for outside the walls of one's city there was indeed danger and fear of the unknown. There were no cell phones, no paved roads (if there were roads at all), no highway police, no signs and road maps. There were lurking thieves, inns that harbored potential bandits and murderers waiting for the pious pilgrim to stop for a night's rest. Therefore, if one did not travel with companions (or if one was wealthy or noble, with a retinue of knights), then the probability of the pilgrim ever reaching the longed-for destination and returning home again was practically nil.

Granted there were protections and places of sanctuary (churches and monasteries, in particular) for pilgrims, but these provided only minimal, temporary protection. There was also the distinctive garb that set the pilgrim apart. The London preacher, Richard Alkerton, declared in 1406, "The pilgrim shall array himself. And then he oweth first to make himself bemarked with a cross. . . . Afterwards the pilgrim shall have a staff, a sclavein, and a scrip." The staff consisted of a tough wooden stick with a metal toe, the sclavein was a long, coarse tunic, the scrip a soft pouch, usually made of leather, strapped to the pilgrim's waist; in it the pilgrim kept food and money. This was the pilgrim's attire after the eleventh-century. By the mid thirteenth-century, pilgrims also began to wear a great broad-brimmed hat, turned up at the front, and attached at the back to a long scarf which wound round the body as far as the waist.

All of this was meant to distinguish the pilgrim from the ordinary traveler or adventurer. The pilgrim was an anointed person, one on a holy journey with the blessing and under the protection of the Church. But this very garb and designation made the pilgrim an obvious target for the unscrupulous thief or murderer, or for the Islamic warriors, who thought they could secure their hold on

Jerusalem and the Holy Land by stopping the flow of Christian pilgrims and the knights who sometimes attended them.

How dangerous, then, and uncertain was the medieval pilgrim way, a danger recognized by both Church and State. Again Richard Alkerton: "He that be a pilgrim oweth first to pay his debts, afterwards set his house in governance, and afterwards to array himself and take his leave of his neighbors, and so go forth."

According to Jonathan Sumption the pilgrim's first act was to make a will. Pilgrims were given the privilege of disposing of their property by will, a privilege which until the late Middle Ages, was accorded only to a few.

Because a pilgrimage should be a journey of poverty, pilgrims made donations to the poor and ceded their property to others. Upon their return they might only have the usufruct of but not the possession of their former property. True pilgrims were to make amends to all they might have offended. Those who left without making amends to people they had wronged could not make a good sacramental confession, without which the pilgrimage was considered worthless.

Once his or her enemies were placated and creditors satisfied, the pilgrim sought out the parish priest, or occasionally the bishop, for a formal blessing. Blessing ceremonies reflected the growing feeling among pilgrims that they belonged to a special "order" of the church, distinguished from others by a uniform and a solemn ritual of initiation.

In a very real sense, medieval pilgrimage was a matter of life and death, with the scales tipped toward death, given the probability that the pilgrim would never return. Pilgrimage was a rehearsal for death—the letting go, the surrender to the unknown, the response to God's beckoning call. The pilgrim who did return was like one who has had a near-death experience and now looks at life from the "other side."

Pilgrimage was like martyrdom, or like Christ's own *Via Crucis*, His Way of the Cross, his willingness to lay down his life trusting in the Father's love. Pilgrimage was the lay person's asceticism, an asceticism as rigorous as the monk's or nun's spiritual discipline. Pilgrims, like monk and nuns, at least for a time had to live with others who were not of their own choosing.

All this rigor and spiritual discipline, of course, was the ideal. Many pilgrimages were in reality little less than traveling bands of merry-makers, and at times, lusty feasts of love "on the road." For like life itself (of which pilgrimage is supposed to be an image), there are good and bad and lukewarm people on pilgrimage; there is chaff among the wheat. For the true pilgrim this means that there was and is the further complication of traveling at times with less than spiritually motivated companions. Thus, purity of heart, requires what life itself requires: faith, hope and charity, and the cardinal virtues of prudence, justice, fortitude, and temperance to counteract the seven capital sins: pride, envy, anger, sloth, avarice, gluttony, and lust.

Pilgrimage is really an intensification of life itself. We choose to go on pilgrimage as a way of embracing the journey of every soul's journey into God. Pilgrimage, then, is an image of what the journey of life is about. That, I believe, is the reason it endures—not because of relics and shrines, but because we sense intuitively that this holy journey is a rehearsal for death and resurrection. We go on pilgrimage to see our life in miniature, to walk physically and geographically the journey of the soul to God.

If and when the pilgrim returns home, he or she is not looking at the hesitant person still standing, one foot in and one foot out of the city gate. The pilgrim's eyes are turned heavenward in gratitude, singing with Psalm 44:

> For not in my bow do I trust,
> nor can my sword save me.
> But you have saved us from our foes,
> and have put to confusion those who hate us.
> In God we have boasted continually,
> and we will give thanks to your name forever.
> (*vs.* 6–8)

❊ *Yearning for Home*

L ike Dante's narrator in *The Divine Comedy*, when
we begin our pilgrimage, we want only to return
home. Despite all the eagerness, the intensity, the desire
to reach the destination, there is an inevitable homesickness
that accompanies us. Sometimes this feeling is pronounced
and leads to sadness or even to tears. At other times it is
more subtle. We try to find home even when we are
somewhere else. We may, for example, keep trying to
find the kind of food that we enjoyed at home. Or we
look for the same kinds of entertainment or diversions,
even though we're in a very different culture with a
different cuisine, and unfamiliar entertainment. As
strong as the temptation to give up on the pilgrimage and
go home may be, we learn to move beyond the feelings
of homesickness and concentrate, as much as possible,
on the goal of reaching the destination. We imagine the
destination. We see it as clearly as we can in order to
allow the dream of arrival, the dream of purification or
transformation, the dream of grace or healing to move us
forward no matter how strong or weak, no matter how
evident or subtle the temptation to return home
becomes.

So, as pilgrims we experience ambivalence from the very beginning. There is the longing to go somewhere else in order to be transformed; to go somewhere better physically, emotionally, and spiritually than where we live now. On the other hand, there is the longing to be at home, the very place that is "sending us forth," beckoning us to go beyond the place we call home to another place—a place we believe will help us return home and live better than we are living now.

All of this shows us again that the dynamic of pilgrimage is the very dynamic of the human soul, the human person. We are both comfortable and uncomfortable with where we are. We are both comfortable and uncomfortable with who we are. We move between these two poles: We want to stay, we want to leave. We want to remain in a given state of being, and we want to move beyond that state. Pilgrimage, therefore, mirrors the very stuff of life, what it means to be human, to be somewhere, some place, and also to want to move beyond that place. We long to find something beyond who and where we are right now and which somehow fulfills what our present place does not. So we move forward in ambiguity, while looking backward at the same time.

This spiritual journey also involves leaving something behind. It involves letting go, trusting that what we love will somehow be okay without our being there. Pilgrimage from the very beginning, and of its very nature, involves surrender—surrender to a power beyond ourselves, a power we trust in, a power we are both leaving behind to care for those we love and that at the same time is drawing us away from them to another place that will help us better relate and love.

✳ *Traveling in Ordinary Time*

The way of the pilgrim can be dangerous, but it can also be boring. Sometimes, there are days when there is nothing but movement, a sense of one's feet moving, or the plane or car moving, or the train moving— the rails clicking, the wheels turning. The pilgrim seems to feel nothing or even to see nothing. That again is a challenge, as it is for the person who looks at the landscape of his or her life and doesn't see all the marvels in it.

Our pilgrim soul can be so fixed on the destination, on the anticipation of some grand experience at the end of the pilgrimage that we do not really see all the wonders along the way. The challenge is not to be bored. The landscape itself is not boring; it is we who are bored. We don't have enough vision to see the beauty around us to see the beauty in things—to see the variety, even though the landscape might at first seem to be monotonously the same.

As I write these words, I am on an Amtrak train between Albuquerque, New Mexico, and Las Vegas, New Mexico. I've made this journey many times,

beginning from when I was fifteen years old and took the
Santa Fe Railroad's *El Capitan* from Gallup via Chicago,
on my journeys back and forth from Gallup to the seminary in Cincinnati.

It is early October, and I've forgotten how many
deciduous trees there are along the way. I was anticipating
pine trees, piñon trees, fir and spruce, and they are here.
But there are also many aspen trees and scrub oak now
turning yellow and orange, the quaking aspens trembling
as if shivering from the slight chill in the air in anticipation
of losing those same leaves, of winter coming.

I had forgotten, too, how much land there is in New
Mexico, and the ancient feel of the land. I remember stories
that I heard as a boy, of the old Franciscan missionaries on
the Navajo reservation and in northern New Mexico,
riding horseback or trudging over the land for miles and
miles just to visit a small mission place or a hacienda to
celebrate Mass, to administer the sacraments. I wonder
what went through the minds of those early missionaries
as they slowly moved across the land. What stories did
they remember? Did they draw upon sacred Scripture for
sustenance? Did they recall the Jewish people in the
desert? Did they remember Abraham being called from
the land of Ur to go into the wilderness? Or did they just
look dully at the landscape, at the sky?

It was probably a little of both. And that is the way
of the pilgrim. Not every day or every journey is an
emotional high, a time of excitement and wonder. Some
days are like the liturgical calendar itself, ordinary days,
ordinary time—a time for just looking at the landscape,
whether it's the landscape of our soul, of the church year,
or of the actual landscape of the earth. That too is pilgrimage; that too is healing—healing of our eyes, healing for

our soul. Just to look, to receive the images that are passing by—the tranquility and peace of the distant horizon, can be a healing experience.

So much of the landscape is invested with events, with stories we do not know. We can pass them by, dismiss them as we plod along looking for something more exciting ahead, or we can look and wonder about who lived in that abandoned house. What caused those cattle skulls to lie bleached and white in the sun? Places are rich in memory; if not our memory, then the memory of others. The memory, perhaps, of a whole people. Who were these Native Americans whose ruins I see from the train window? What were their dreams? Where did they go on pilgrimage? What were their sacred places? What stories do they tell about those places? What wisdom is in those places, in the stories that are told, in the events that happened there?

Ordinary time becomes transformed, and we ask: What is the story of my pilgrimage? What events take place as I move through life—as I move across the land and the ocean? These are the questions that deepen the journey itself and not just the experience of reaching the destination. These are the questions that transform ordinary time into extraordinary time.

I am making these reflections, asking these questions returning from my parents' graves. My parents are buried in Payson, Arizona, and once a year no matter where I am, I try to make a pilgrimage to their graves, not just to reverence their relics, not just to prayerfully remember their lives and our lives together, but also to make the pilgrimage back to my childhood that each one of us makes, a trip from which we return a different person each time. There are years I don't want to make the journey because it seems too hard to remember how long ago it was we lived together and how long ago it was that they died.

A pilgrimage back to our parents' graves is also, if it's made as mine is, once a year, a time for reviewing our life. Perhaps there have been mostly ordinary times, but when viewed in perspective, looking back over a whole year, certain seemingly ordinary days will stand out when we ask: What has happened from the time we last stood or knelt at their graves?

It's a time of review and a time for examining our conscience. How have we grown? Where has God led us in these intervening months? What has been the wisdom God has given us? What suffering, what sorrow, what loss has bound us closer to Christ, the poor crucified Savior who walked the earth as we walk the earth, whose life too was a pilgrimage, from heaven to earth and back again. How is it that Christ's life has transformed our lives, made extraordinary what seemed at the time just ordinary time? We see that ordinary time is extraordinary when lived in God, and the extraordinary is really ordinary.

✳ *Ritual*

The pilgrim's journey, as I discover each time I go to my parents' graves, is not just a journey to that sacred place, to those relics, but it is also a journey into myself, revealing more subtle and deeper levels each time I go, each time I recall the meaning of that year's journey. Each time I go to my parents' graves I hope that I'm bringing them a self that has grown a bit. I try to ritualize that growth, that change, by the kind of flowers I bring this time, by the prayers that I say which are perhaps different from the year before, by a further reconciliation with something in our shared pasts that still needs reconciling.

In all pilgrimage, ritual is important. Ritualizing the experience makes it something more than cerebral. Rather it affects the whole person. I have a friend who each year on the anniversary of his wife's death, goes to her grave with some friends where they ritually pour Bombay gin on her grave because she liked Martinis. As frivolous as that may seem, there is something in libation, a pouring out that symbolizes a pouring out of the soul, a pouring out of love, of remembrance. There is extravagance in my friend's ritual because gin, especially Bombay gin, is expensive; it's not something that one normally pours into the ground.

In the annual ritual of spilling gin on the grave there is also the dimension of community. My friend goes with others who knew his wife, who laughed with her, who celebrated with her, who worshiped with her. They together make the pilgrimage. Therefore there is a further sense of community, of bonding among them as they make the annual pilgrimage, perhaps one member less through death, perhaps one member absent because he or she has moved to another place, or is ill. Still they go together, however many they are, to celebrate this person's life, to tell stories, to pour out gin, to pray.

✳ *Illness and Pilgrimage*

S ickness itself can be a pilgrimage, one of the most
profound journeys into silence and solitude. Sickness
is one of the most difficult journeys of faith; sickness is
the archetype of journey as pilgrimage.

In the Spring of 1995 I accompanied four people on
a journey of faith and healing: a child with muscular
dystrophy; his parents, themselves broken with worry
and grief for their only child; and a woman in chronic
pain resulting from a botched surgery and its complications. The farther we traveled to the place of healing,
the further we entered into inner healing. The external
journey was to a famed Christian healer. The inner journey
was a pilgrimage into the soul, where God dwells, the
place in which we receive healing and become channels
of healing for each other. We were bringing with us the
very God we were traveling to find.

And thus it is. The traveling *towards* reveals what is
there all along but is not revealed except in reaching out
for it, "going for it," as they say. We run the race only to
discover that the goal is that we've run the race; in
running we discover within what we are running
towards and the source of our ability to run. The healing

is in the pilgrimage, the prayer, regardless of what happens when we arrive. The arrival itself is recursive; it invites us to look back, to assess, to realize what happened on the way. We discover that we were altered by the pilgrimage, as much as by the arrival itself.

A healing pilgrimage is the soul in search of its own healing through bodily ministrations that are soul ministrations and vice versa. Prayer for healing always touches both body and soul, and the very movement toward healing is a movement that involves the body on a pilgrimage into the soul. We may be going to a geographical location, but we are also journeying within. The external journey facilitates the internal.

The small group that made this pilgrimage toward healing did not return with "miraculous" cures, but in everyone some healing was manifest. In the young couple there was increased faith and a return to church and prayer. They began to pray with a small group of believers for continued healing both of their child and of their own hearts. The young woman who seemed to experience only temporary and negligible relief of pain, slowly began to heal over the weeks and months afterwards and continued to pray for healing. Months later she found herself in New York kneeling before the tomb of Terrence Cardinal Cooke in St. Patrick's Cathedral and experienced through his intercession a significant lessening of her pain. The young boy was not miraculously healed, but the progression of his disease was arrested.

All who made the healing pilgrimage lost their discouragement and found the courage and hope to continue pursuing medical help.

What we learned in this small pilgrimage of healing is that there are seldom magical solutions—instant healings in our lives, but there is always the operation of grace, that mysterious gift of Gods' divine life in us drawing us closer to union with God. Grace enables us to surrender to God's will, even when it seems humanly absurd to do so. God does not want us to be sick, yet God, at times, seems to do nothing or little to heal us, just as God failed to heal and deliver from the cross his own Son, who cried out to him, "My God, my God, why have you forsaken me?" (Mt. 27:46b).

God is the Creator, the Redeemer, the Sanctifier. God is free to do what God chooses to do or not to do. We can only be open channels to whatever healing God chooses to work *through us or in us*. We have no claim on God, except that of the creature before the Creator— an infinite distance that only God can bridge as God chooses.

It is the eternal question of the suffering of Job. The only answer is that of Job himself, who recognizes that God can do whatever God wills; for though God is all powerful, God's power is not at our command but God's.   Job says:

I know that you can do all things,
and that no purpose of yours can be thwarted.
Who is this that hides counsel without knowledge?
Therefore I have uttered what I did not understand,
things too wonderful for me, which I did not know.
(*Job 42:2-3*)

Whenever we approach and try to articulate the deepest questions of life, we are in the realm of mystery. All we can do is surrender to the mystery, by trying not to become bitter or resentful, and not to reject a God who does not do what we would have God do. God is free as we are free. Only unconditional love can unite free beings.

How facile the above words must seem to someone who is suffering or dying. These words, like the words of Job's friends, are but intellectual exercises while words of pain and anger directed at God, questioning words, are true and real, just as Job's were. At the end of the Book of Job God does not commend Job's friends for defending God; rather God defends the honesty of Job. God says to Eliphaz, "My wrath is kindled against you and against your two friends; for you have not spoken of me what is right, as my servant Job has." (Job 42:7b) Job speaks truthfully what he feels, but in the end he surrenders to God's will. "I despise myself, and repent in dust and ashes." (Job 42:6)

The words of this chapter have been written without pain and seem to me therefore unworthy of a reader's pain and suffering, of one who may be looking to them for some hope, some comfort and consolation. Words fail here. We don't understand why some are in pain and suffering. We don't know why God doesn't heal some of us—why some are healed on their pilgrimage to miraculous shrines like the Shrine of Our Lady of Lourdes in France, and some are not. We do know God loves us and will bring us to wholeness, if not here, then in eternity. We do know that sooner or later the journey of sickness is everybody's story. That may be small comfort to one who is in pain or illness, but it is ultimately all we know.

Our mini word-pilgrimage has now brought us to this point of honesty which is the place where love and forgiveness can begin, the first movement toward the healing of the heart. What is more, this story of a healing pilgrimage invites us to make our own journeys of healing, whether into the heart or to a place of healing. In the journey itself there is healing if not of the body, then of the soul; if not a mending of the body, then a mending of the heart. In faith's journey itself there is a further wholeness, a peace that is the grace of making the pilgrimage toward healing.

PART TWO

The Pilgrim's Credo

I *am not in control.*
I *am not in a hurry.*
I *walk in faith and hope.*
I *greet everyone with peace.*
I *bring back only what God gives me.*

✳ A Pilgrimage to Rome and Assisi

A cold wind blows into New York the day of our sailing—a cold wind, intermittent rain, and a gray sky are reminiscent of eighteenth century Dutch paintings of sailing vessels huddled together just beyond the beach from which intrepid sailors are embarking in small rowboats that will take them out to the brave sailing ships.

And so the journey and quest begin. Luckily we are not embarking on a sailing ship; we are walking up the gangplank of a modern diesel-driven ship. Radar and other instruments have already forewarned us of a storm heading toward Nova Scotia. There's also a gale farther out in the North Atlantic. The captain has adjusted our passage accordingly, charting our course directly east, far south of Nova Scotia and the Grand Banks where the seas are often rougher because of the shallower fishing waters there.

As soon as we pass under the Verrazano Narrows Bridge and move out into open water, the ship begins to roll slightly, a movement that increases during the night so that by 6:30 AM when I begin to take laps around the deck, I'm swaying from side to side, wondering if it will get worse as the day wears on. I look at the navigational chart posted on the bulletin board and observe that our plotted course continues directly east for many miles before finally arcing northward in the Great Circle Route that is the shortest distance to Southampton.

All 1700 of us on this grand ship are more dependent on the moods of the sea and the weather than we would like to think. We are certainly less in control than we would be back home.

Assisi, St. Francis, and St. Clare are the beacons drawing me onward, even with rough seas and long quarter swells and the possibility of catching the southern end of a gale. The low-pressure system is too broad and deep to avoid the gale altogether, and so, as I often do at the beginning of a retreat, instead of diving headlong into the book I've been waiting to read, I sleep. Because there's no other means of escape, I surrender to the tiredness I've brought with me.

By morning we are parting the waters into the edge of a gale. For twenty-four hours twenty-five foot waves and fifty knot winds buffet the ship. Images of Christ's disciples caught in a storm at sea rise in my mind as well as images of St. Paul and St. Francis shipwrecked and driven ashore. Images, too, of the Franciscan nuns drowned at sea in a storm, whose death was the occasion of Gerard Manley Hopkins's great poem, "The Wreck of the Deutschland." The way to God is fraught with danger, detour, and death.

In my own case, we passed safely through the gale, and the whole experience of crossing the ocean by ship was full and rich. I discovered that few geographies so perfectly mirror a pilgrimage as a sea passage: the surrender to elements surpassingly superior to anything you can control; the mystery, the danger, the sheer magnitude of the undertaking—the sense of participating in a journey thousands and thousands of years old. Even with the modern technology of ship-building, with weather-forecasting and communication, a sea passage evokes primal depths: your small bark on vast waters—the pitching and rolling—the silence—the night bright with stars and moonlight—the monotonous horizon—the volatile sea-god Poseidon lurking beneath calm waters—all hint of pilgrimage.

As we sailed out of New York harbor, passing Ellis Island and the Statue of Liberty with her familiar torch held aloft against the setting sun, I felt a small surface tremor. Something was shifting within me. I saw my paternal and maternal grandparents, my father at three years of age, all huddled together somewhere on Ellis Island, their eyes wide with fear and hope, hoping that Colorado was on the horizon. How many days was their passage—a month-long passage from Genoa to New York? Mine would be shorter, six days to Southampton.

As in a movie reel reversing, I watched the tip of Manhattan, the Statue of Liberty, recede. Something was unwinding, rewinding within me. I looked down at the sea swells. I looked back at Ellis Island. I sensed the inner shift. I prayed both passages would be safe.

The sea voyage I'm sketching here is a metaphor of life, as all our journeys are. For example, there are allegories written about the pilgrimage to St. James of Compostella in Spain that liken crossing the plain of Leon to the dark night of the soul. Our essential pilgrimage is of the soul, and the external, geographical pilgrimage is a metaphor—an acting out of the yearning and journey of the soul. God himself called the great Biblical personages to leave home and journey forth into the unknown: Abraham and Sarah leaving the land of Ur to a land God would show them; Moses and the Hebrews called to wander the desert for forty years in search of the Promised Land; Jesus himself going on pilgrimage from heaven to earth and back again.

The spiritual leaders of the Bible experience exile and wandering in response to the call of God. Even Mary, the Mother of Jesus, fled with her husband Joseph and the child Jesus into Egypt, thus replicating the journey of Joseph, the son of Jacob, who was sold into slavery by his own brothers.

There is no lasting city here, these journeys seem to say; the way to heaven is the way of the pilgrim and stranger. "How lovely is your dwelling place, O Lord of hosts!" the Psalmist sings (Ps. 84:1).

Of course, we need not all be geographical pilgrims; we can travel in our own place. The history of monasteries has proven how deep is the inner journey of the rooted person. Simeon, in the New Testament, went only as far as the temple every day, and there the Incarnate God came to him.

The inner journey of the rooted person has its own perils and dangers and a turbulence as frightening as the outward journey of making a sea passage. In the same way, an actual passage across water, land, or in the air can replicate and even trigger inward passages similar to the outer passage we are making.

"To each," as they say, "one's own." There are many ways to go to God. Pilgrimage is both vertical and horizontal—often simultaneously. When you travel on pilgrimage to a sacred shrine, you discover that you are making a deep inward journey, as well; or in journeying deeply inward where you are rooted, you find yourself journeying with Abraham or Moses or Jesus.

❋ The Way to Rome

1.

Loneliness is often our companion, even at times when we travel with others. No matter how focused we might be on a sacred destination, there are days when we travel "alone," when we feel cut off from home and loved ones, and we want to turn around and go back. We can find reasons enough to justify going back, including rationalizations about how much better we pray at home, how much more centered we are there.

Today, riding the train from London to Dover, feels like one of those days. I've just said good-bye to friends in London. The long stretch to Dover, then on across the Channel to Calais, and from there to Paris and Geneva, as I make my way to Rome to meet other pilgrims for our journey to Assisi, seems an interminable trip. I'm on a local train, besides, stopping at Bromley South, St. Mary Croy, Swanley, Farmingham Road, Longfield, Meopham, Sole Street, Rochester, Chatham, Gillingham, Rainham, Newington, Sittingbourne, Teynham, Faversham, Canterbury East, Selling, Bekesbourne, Adisham, Aylesham, Snowdown, Shepherdswell, Kearnsey, and Dover Priory.

I discover, however, that instead of wearing me out this seemingly endless litany of quaint names reminds me of medieval pilgrims who walked through village after English village, making their way from London to Canterbury's shrine of the martyred Bishop, St. Thomas a Becket. My heart lifts with each name and my eyes look out to the countryside farms, to the horses and cows, the sheep and goats scattered here and there across the landscape. Beauty is all around me, though I seem more aware of who is not here and why I've come so far from home. I'm hoping that my pilgrimage will once again reach God's heart; and the world, like this scene outside my window, will be transformed, as it has been on other pilgrimages, and I'll see the familiar world of home in a whole new light and embrace it with a renewed love.

2.

Just as St. Francis dismounted from his horse and embraced a leper and found God in his arms, so the pilgrim today longs for that moment when the face of God is revealed. Will that revelation come through another person or persons, as it did for St. Francis; or will it come through nature as it is doing now as we admire the mountains surrounding us as we travel from Geneva to Milan through Lausanne, Montreux, Sion, Brig, Domodossola, and Stresa?

The Alps are snow-capped in late June, their frozen summits emphasizing that their ascent is beyond our ability to climb, like the ascent to God. What angels and messengers must help us to ascend to such heights, or even when we find the heights here below in the descent into all of creation in imitation of Christ, who, as St. Paul tells us in his letter to the Philippians, "though he was in the form of God, did not regard equality with God as something to be exploited, but emptied himself, taking the form of a slave, being born in human likeness" (Phil. 2:6-7a).

With the help of saints and angels we ascend the mountain in order to descend again purified as St. Francis was purified when he ascended to mountain hermitages to pray and then returned a renewed person, better able to witness to the God revealed to him on the mountain top.

The God of the mountain top and the God of the plains and valleys below is the same God, but we are transformed through the journey up the mountain and back down again to the plain. The outer landscape becomes a mirror image of the inner. In climbing a mountain, we climb something inside ourselves; every crossing of landscape or seascape is a crossing of something inside us; every tracing of a labyrinth untangles something inside our tangled soul; every descent is a descent into the soul if we are aware of it and surrender to the mystery of the complementarity of inner and outer realities.

Even lifting our eyes to the mountains, as I do now towards the Matterhorn in Brig, Switzerland, lifts us up and away from our winding progress through the mountain valley. I want to stay here in awe of the mountain and not go on to the blazing heat of Rome only to begin another phase of the pilgrimage, but the pilgrim's way is to move on, surrendering to the relentless movement toward one's destination.

I look out the window at the gray streams of melting snow and granite tailings. How many stones must this murky water pass over and through before it emerges a clear mountain stream!

Tunnels. We enter a long train tunnel between Brig and Iselle, followed by another shorter tunnel and then a long one again and another short one, in and out of light and darkness. What is our experience of subterranean tunnels? Why does our breath sometimes shorten? What is our fear? The fear begins when we attend to the tunnel itself instead of the passage through to the light—in this case, into Italy, the land of sun.

To pass through the tunnel is an act of faith that light is there beyond, and even within the tunnel, though light may be hidden temporarily. The light at the end of the tunnel is what makes the passage bearable—the darkness will not last.

But we do not know this in the depths of darkness; we can only believe it on the testimony of those who have made the passage before us.

3.

I am at last in Rome, exiting the Termini, the main train station. My first encounter is with a beggar as I stand in line waiting for a taxi, a beggar I immediately, instinctively, refuse, lest I commit the egregious error of reaching for my wallet and reveal to everyone where I keep it. I know from past experience that you must be prepared, money in hand, if you're going to give alms to a beggar. Otherwise, like all the pilgrims before you, you're an easy target for pickpockets and thieves, one of whom might be the very beggar standing before you.

And so my time in Rome begins—Rome the impossible, the city that invites charity and goodness and then subverts it with all those who prey upon pilgrims and tourists. I came this time hoping to be like St. Francis: talk with the beggars, learn their names, give them what I could, but habit, knowledge, tiredness, and wanting to get to my *pensione* prevented me again. Was I being wise or was I rationalizing away a possible encounter with God? Did I miss an opportunity to change, to be transformed by the "Beggar-God" whom we so often meet along the way in the guise of people who seem to wear anything but the face of the God we were expecting?

I have heard advice to pilgrims over the years: *Lacking the language, as you probably do, being in a country and culture foreign to you, it's best to go into any church in Rome and put the money in the poor box there. "Per i Poveri," for the poor, will be marked on the box; and those there will know how and to whom to distribute the money.*

Through the centuries chroniclers of pilgrim journeys have warned pilgrims to be careful of those who accost them for alms—it may be a ploy to rob them, then or later. And so the real poor go uncared for and neglected, except by those who've dedicated themselves to serving them. I tell myself, here in Rome, that the churches know who these servants of the poor are (and I'm probably right), and they will be sure my alms are well distributed. That, at least, is my trust.

But I enter my taxi feeling uncomfortable; I think about the beggar. I wonder what would have happened had I broken through my caution and "common sense" and done something rash, like reaching for money and giving it to her? What would St. Francis have done?

4.

All my years in Rome and Assisi have made me aware of feet, and how important they are to the pilgrim who does so much walking, mindful that he or she is walking in the footsteps of Christ who walked the earth before us. Our feet kiss the earth made holy by the feet of Jesus: they ache as his feet ached; they accumulate dirt and grime; they become blistered; they bleed and they need attending to.

Pilgrims begin with an experience as mundane and humanly shared as feet. His feet, first of all, the God-man, who walked into the desert and emerged to step into the Jordan River to be baptized by his cousin, John; who walked through the towns and villages of Judea and Galilee; who walked on water; walked to the Garden of Gethsemani, to the high priest's house, to the Praetorium of the Roman governor, Pontius Pilate, to the palace of King Herod; who walked the stones of the way of Calvary—to Golgotha, the Place of the Skull, outside Jerusalem; who walked from the tomb, walked through closed doors where the disciples were gathered; walked the road to Emmaus and many other roads for forty days before ascending into heaven, his feet disappearing into the clouds. His feet, too, according to the ancient legend, walked the Appian Way toward Rome, causing Peter, who was leaving the city, to ask Jesus, "*Quo vadis?*" "Where are you going, Lord?" When Jesus answered, "I am going to Rome to be crucified again," Peter turned around and re-entered Rome to be crucified upside down in deference to his Savior and Lord, whose footprints remain in stone at the Church of "Quo Vadis" at a crossroads of the Appian Way.

The pilgrim way is that concrete. We may walk with our heads in the clouds, but the very means of our walking is grounded in the earth. Heaven and earth are the two dimensions of pilgrimage conjoined in a journey that involves the whole person, body, soul, and spirit. This wholeness is one of the great values of pilgrimage; it keeps us from an idealized, ethereal notion of holiness; it de-cosmeticizes our life in God.

5.

My way is directed by the Rule of St. Francis, the shortest rule in the Church. This rule, a sort of guidebook intended for poor itinerant brothers, is my manual for the road. St. Francis says in chapter III, "I advise, admonish, and exhort you in the Lord Jesus Christ that when you travel through the world, you do not quarrel or argue or judge others; rather be meek, peaceful and modest, courteous and humble, speaking honorably to everyone."

How wise these words are, for there is always something you don't know, and some way of doing things that causes embarrassment when you presume to know. In Italy, for example, you presume your Eurail pass is good on all trains, but if you travel on small local or regional railways, you are told by the conductor that your Eurail is worthless (with a "tsk, tsk," and a wave of the finger); it is good only on Italian State Railways. If you board a state railway that happens to be a Euro Star train and fail to pre-register for a reservation, thus failing to pay the supplement required for an assigned seat, you again will be embarrassed (Why didn't I read the Eurail brochure more carefully?) and may have to stand if the train is full.

In a bar or restaurant, you must go first to the *Cassa* (cash register) and pay for whatever you want, receive a ticket, and then go to the counter for your coffee, *panini* (sandwich), or whatever.

Submitting with good humor to these realities on the way is good discipline for accepting deeper, more wounding rejections and disappointments. Such small inconveniences prepare the pilgrim for what St. Francis called "perfect joy" in the following, gospel-like parable:

St. Francis summoned Brother Leo and said, "Brother Leo, are you ready to take down some words?" He answered, "I am ready."

"Write, then, this story about true joy: A messenger comes and says that all the teachers of the University of Paris have entered our Order—write that this is not true joy. Or so have all the prelates north of the Alps, and the archbishops and bishops as well, or the King of France and the King of England, too—write that neither is this true joy. Or if he announces that my brothers have gone among nonbelievers and converted them all to the faith, or that I have so much divine grace that I heal the sick and perform miracles—I tell you, Brother Leo, none of these things is true joy. . . ."

"Father Francis, what then is true and perfect joy?"

"Well, I am returning to Perugia, say, and I arrive at our Friary of the Porziuncola very late at night. It is wintertime, muddy, and so cold that icicles have gathered at the fringes of my habit and keep cutting into my legs until they bleed. But at last, cold and covered with mud, I make it to the entrance of the Porziuncola. I knock and knock and call out, and finally a brother comes and asks, 'Who are you?' and when I answer, 'Brother Francis,' he says, "Go away. This isn't the hour to be wandering about. How dare you want to come in!' And when I insist, he snaps back, 'Get out of here, you simpleton, you idiot! We have brothers enough here and we don't need one more like you.' But I again move toward the door and say, 'For the love of God, please take me in tonight.' 'Absolutely not!' he says. 'Go to the Crosiers' hostel and ask them.'"

"Now I tell you this: If I keep my patience through all this and do not get upset, then that is true joy and true virtue and salvation of soul."

�֍ St. Peter's Basilica, the Tomb of Blessed John XXIII

Entering into silence. Closing my eyes. Descending to the center. Silence. Then they surface, the names of people and places I want to bring to this prayer. I kneel before the remains of Blessed John XXIII in the shiny glass case beneath the altar of St. Jerome in St. Peter's Basilica. His waxed remains, like a supine figure in a wax museum, lie just behind and below the ancient statue of St. Peter, its foot worn smooth by the touches and kisses of countless pilgrims to Rome.

St. Peter and Blessed John XXIII are two men who listened and were not afraid to act—two who said outrageous things. It's appropriate somehow that they should be so closely linked in this great house of God.

I can pray here, even though uninterrupted lines of the devout and the curious pass before me as they pray or gawk and then move on to the next shrine or curiosity. I can pray here because prayer is happening all around me, and because I know this blessed man is listening, even as I pray not to him, but to God through his intercession.

Why is it we seek the intercession of the saints? Will not God hear us as willingly? I've never known a better answer than that it's easier to go begging with someone who knows how, someone we know is more practiced than we are at receiving alms—more practiced and more generous than we are because they gave to others what they received from God; they gave to people like us when they were among us. They'll do the same, we believe, now that they're receiving more love than they can ever retain.

Angelo Roncalli, good Pope John, was and is that kind of man. It's easy to pray here; I almost expect an answer with a twist of humor, as when he was the new smiling Pope with a twinkle in his eye who said, "If you only knew what God is about to do through me, a peasant from Bergamo."

You did the seemingly impossible once; I believe you'll do it again for me and all these pray-ers who file by your glass coffin, hoping, hoping. . . .

✳ *The Recurring Pilgrimage*

I don't remember if it was raining that first March night in Assisi, as it often was in the spring of 1972. I do remember the address of St. Anthony's Guest House: Via Galeazzo Alessi 10, 06081 Assisi (PG), Italy. I was to live there for three months working on my first book, *Francis, the Journey and the Dream.* I remember Sister Maria, who died of cancer a few years later, and Sister Rosita, who still resides there, and some of the guests who passed through, like the Antons from Iowa and Bertie Lomas from London, who became life-long friends of mine.

Though my stay in Assisi was grounded at St. Anthony's, I was still a pilgrim living outside a Franciscan Friary at the direction of my Father Provincial, who felt St. Anthony's would give me the time and freedom I needed to write—which it did.

I can still see the small room at the end of the corridor, its narrow bed shoved close against the wall, the mini-writing table on which a portable Olivetti typewriter rested. The only other object on the desk was my *"quaderno,"* a notebook which contained my handwritten work of the day waiting to be typed on the Olivetti that I had rented in nearby Perugia. This typewriter gave me fits at the beginning because the Italian keyboard is slightly different from the American keyboard I was used to, thus working havoc with the touch system I'd learned in high school.

Next to the desk was a sink and a mirror, and across the corridor was a toilet and bath. I learned to take sponge baths at the small sink those cold Spring days. For a couple of hours on Saturday evening there was hot water for a bath. All of this appealed somehow to my pilgrim heart, as did helping serve guests in the dining room.

After daily Mass in the chapel, I would take breakfast and then write all morning in longhand. In the afternoon after siesta I would read the morning's writing and then type it up as a second draft. The following morning I would read this before I began writing the next longhand pages.

It was a peaceful rhythm of writing and reading and re-writing on the Olivetti. At the end of the week I would duplicate all the typed pages. The whole process was slow and thoughtful.

Evenings after supper I would walk down to the Piazza Commune and have a cappuccino as I sat at an outdoor table watching the young people singing and dancing and the citizens of Assisi taking their evening *passeggiata*, a stroll, through the piazza. It was an idyllic three months in a mystical city that enchanted and became my muse.

❋ ❋ ❋ ❋

That experience in Assisi in 1972 became a rich fund of experience and memory that I continue to draw upon and which draws me back to Assisi. Such is often the case with pilgrims who return to the same place again and again. They try to re-create the original experience. My first pilgrimage to Assisi was a revelation of the story of Francis himself, and I return, as others have done and continue to do, in order to re-learn his story chapter by chapter, a story that yields ongoing insights into the pilgrim way to God.

Like the modern pilgrim Francis was born into a world of wars. Pope and Emperor warred against each other; non-unified Italian city-states warred among themselves for the lands surrounding their walled cities. Francis was born in 1182 in one of those city-states, the Umbrian town of Assisi. We know him today as a man of peace and love. How did he move through all the violence of his time and maintain the image of the person we all associate with the famous peace prayer attributed to him? It is a prayer in the heart of anyone who would go on pilgrimage or live as a humble pilgrim in this world.

> Lord, make me an instrument of your peace.
> Where there is hatred let me sow love,
> Where there is injury pardon,
> Where there is doubt faith,
> Where there is despair hope,
> Where there is darkness light,
> And where there is sadness joy.
> O Divine Master,
> Grant that I may not so much
> Seek to be consoled as to console,
> To be understood as to understand,
> To be loved as to love.

For it is in giving that we receive,
It is in pardoning that we are pardoned,
And it is in dying that we are born to eternal life.

Though Francis himself did not write this prayer, it is consistently attributed to him because it sums up his life—the way he walked through the world.

He did not begin that way. He was the rich son of the cloth merchant, Pietro Bernardone, and his wife, the Lady Pica. He was baptized "John" when his father was away on a cloth-buying trip in France. When his father returned, he changed his son's name to Francesco, the Frenchman.

Francis, true to his name, grew up enamored of the French language and of the tales of the knights and ladies of the French romances. He was a carefree boy, generous and fun-loving, pursuing life with gusto, partying and carousing with his friends.

Not a prudish or pious killjoy, Francis was the kind of person who attracted the people around him as he continues to do today—the life of the party, the one who made things happen. Throughout the levity of his younger years, Francis dreamed of becoming a knight, a romantic dream certainly, because in reality this was a serious, bloody enterprise. When war broke out between Assisi and the neighboring town of Perugia, Francis rode off to war as a knight, only to be captured in the very first skirmish.

A year of imprisonment in Perugia changed him deeply. He was only twenty-one years old, but he returned to Assisi a broken man, lying ill in bed for a whole year. When he finally recovered he again went to war in the papal army battling the forces of the Holy Roman Emperor, but God had other plans and in a vision instructed Francis to return to Assisi where it would be revealed what he was to do. Francis listened to the voice of his dream and returned to Assisi.

One day when he was praying before the crucifix in the dilapidated little chapel of San Damiano, he received his call from God. The crucifix spoke: "Francis, go and repair my house which, as you see, is falling into ruin."

This vision changed Francis's life. He began to build, to repair; not tear down with weapons of destruction. He begged for stones and repaired the run-down chapel, which Francis thought was the "house" the voice was referring to. It *was* this house, but it was more—it was the larger house of the Catholic Church itself that he was to repair.

Francis learned of this larger implication of the vision one day when he saw a leper on the road, impulsively jumped from his horse, gave coins to the leper and embraced him. Francis was stunned that rather than being repulsed he was filled with joy. He came to realize that this was because he had embraced his Lord Jesus Christ.

Shortly afterwards Francis rejected his father's world and went to live among the lepers. Others followed him and the Franciscan movement began.

That is the essence of the story of Francis of Assisi. In Assisi all the details are filled in each time the pilgrim returns and visits another place of Francis and his Brothers, or of the first Franciscan woman, St. Clare, and her Sisters. The Assisi pilgrimage is the unfolding of the story of St. Francis and St. Clare and, because their lives touch our pilgrim hearts, we want to return to learn more about what made this man and this woman so full of joy. Every pilgrimage reveals a different aspect of Francis's and Clare's lives because of our emotional and spiritual states at a given time.

There are as many motivations for returning to Assisi as there are reasons for going on any pilgrimage. We rediscover the mystique and charm of Assisi itself, its medieval ambiance, its people, the vast panorama of the Valley of Spoleto below, and not least, the peace of residing, however briefly, within the walls of the mystical city of St. Francis and St. Clare.

What happened and continues to happen in Assisi comprise not one dramatic occurrence but a constellation of experiences that have a transforming effect. The culture, for example, bids us slow down and live each day a little more fully. The beauty of the mountains, hills, and valleys moves us to praise and gratitude as that same landscape did for Francis and Clare. Of course, the places of these two saints in and around Assisi beckon us to change, to embrace the gospel, to remember what happened here to Francis and Clare and to us when we first came here on pilgrimage. We draw on those memories; we long to return.

✳ *La Maddalena*

Quite near the Basilica of St. Mary of the Angels, on the road to the church of Rivo Torto, is the small, semi-abandoned chapel of La Maddalena (the Magdalen). Here the lepers worshiped; here St. Francis prayed with them. Here, as we know from the very first sentence of his Last Testament, he found his true vocation: "When I was in sins, the sight of lepers nauseated me beyond measure; but then God himself led me into their company, and I worked mercy with them. Once I got to know them, what had nauseated me before became a source of spiritual and physical consolation for me. After that I did not wait long before I left the world."

How is it Francis arrived here? He and his first companions, Bernard of Quintavalle and Peter Catani, had asked the priest of the church of St. Nicholas to open the Gospels for them three times and read what was there, so that they might know God's will for them. This is what they heard:

'If you wish to be perfect, go, sell your possessions and give the money to the poor, and you will have treasure in heaven' (Mt. 19:21).

'Take nothing for your journey' (Lk. 9:3a).

'If any want to become my followers, let them deny themselves, and take up their cross and follow me' (Mt. 16:24).

The call of God through these Gospel passages brought Francis here among the lepers who epitomized and symbolized the gospel person Francis and his followers were to become.

I touch these walls, the walls Francis and the lepers touched, these walls that contained the "cloistered" space where the brothers learned to be Lesser Brothers, poor and dependent on God for the very grace to remain there and minister to those who'd been exiled from society, set apart as unclean.

I touch these walls and wonder how they survived, and I know again that only God can make such a thing happen. But it was St. Francis who took the leap of faith and responded literally to the words of Christ in the Gospel: 'I was hungry and you gave me food, I was thirsty and you gave me something to drink, I was a stranger and you welcomed me, I was naked and you gave me clothing, I was sick and you took care of me, I was in prison and you visited me.' (Mt. 25:35–37). God was there when finally Francis walked out of Assisi and descended the hillside onto the plain where the lepers lived.

I touch these stones and ask for grace, ask to see those fallen by the wayside in our own time; ask for the courage to reach out and touch those who've been rejected, whose lives are lived on the periphery of our lives where we try not to look, not to be involved, not to let ourselves be tainted with what may seem to compromise the respectability we've come to equate with religion.

I touch these stones and wonder what I can do. How can I let God turn the pilgrimage to the sacred places of Francis and Clare into a pilgrimage to those who are invisible: the people who have no place, no spot on earth on which to live; the people who still live in slavery, working for landlords who refuse them not only their freedom but their right to live as human beings; those, including children, who are forced into prostitution and inhuman conditions of work and living.

I touch these stones and pray for all those who are poor and invisible, for those who work with them, for those who support them in any way. I pray for all those who work so devotedly on the local, national, and international levels to raise our consciousness, to transform oppressive systems, to free people from slavery of all kinds.

I touch these stones and ask Jesus to reward those who feed him and give him drink, who visit him in prison and when he is sick, who clothe him—actions which still define what it means to be an authentic Christian.

The very stones are now invested not only with what happened here eight hundred years ago but, through my prayer and the simple ritual of touch, are receiving the heroic work of those who continue to serve the poor and rejected. These stones both give and receive; and, as the other pilgrims with me begin to touch the stones of La Maddalena, I realize they are anointing these stones with their own dreams for a better world, with prayers for and renewed commitment to those who are as invisible as the empty space of this little chapel will be once we leave. Only the stones will remain, but they are enough to remind us of how much we have yet to do to bring justice and peace to the world. These stones cry out to us what St. Francis used to say to his brothers: "Let us begin, Brothers, to serve the Lord, for up to now we have made little or no progress."

❋ The Dormitory of St. Clare

A long time ago I went on a pilgrimage. I didn't know it was a pilgrimage; I was only fourteen years old. I only knew that I was going where God was. It seems naive now, over fifty years later, that I should have thought that going away to a seminary to be a priest was going where God was, but that's what I thought. So I didn't mind at all the 1500 mile bus ride from Gallup to Cincinnati. I was going where God was.

Still I go. I journey long hours and thousands of miles, looking for God. Sometimes I find God, as I did as a young man; sometimes God finds me. Sometimes we miss each other on the road, and so I continue walking. I still go my pilgrim way.

In the Summer of 2003 I walked and traveled by bus with eighteen other pilgrims from Arizona, California, and Jamaica. We walked in the footsteps of St. Francis and St. Clare of Assisi. We began in Assisi and finished in Rome. The walking was hard in the atypically hot June sun. June 11th, they say, was the hottest day in Rome in almost two hundred years. The oppressive, seemingly breezeless heat also lay over Assisi like a hot lid that did not lift, even during what would usually have been cool nights on the side of Mount Subasio. During the day Assisi's pink stone grew as hot as oven bricks under the merciless sun.

"Brother Sun," St. Francis named this same sun. So it proved to be for us. The hotter it got, the warmer grew our hearts, yearning for the fire of God's Spirit to inflame us, transforming what was lukewarm or cold. The outer world seemed to mirror what was happening within, so that we didn't mind and didn't complain, at least about a sun that seemed to be doing more than scorching our faces. Like the sweat that poured from our bodies, impurities flowed out of our hearts as we drew more closely to the Christ of St. Francis and St. Clare, the poor Christ of San Damiano, who spoke to Francis from the crucifix there and who St. Clare called the mirror we are all gradually becoming.

The actual crucifix of San Damiano is now in the Basilica of St. Clare, one of the most precious treasures the Poor Clare Nuns brought with them when they moved from San Damiano, outside the city walls, to the newly completed Basilica of St. Clare. This church was built to house and honor the remains of their founder, the first Franciscan woman, St. Clare.

Though the remains of St. Clare and the crucifix of San Damiano are now in her Basilica, her spirit still remains at San Damiano: in the chapel St. Francis repaired with his own hands, while prophesying that some day poor ladies would live there in the little choir where she and her Sisters prayed; in the refectory where once St. Clare blessed the bread and crosses appeared on each loaf; and most tangibly for me, in the dormitory where she died and where today her healing spirit is still present.

Each year in St. Clare's dormitory there is a healing ritual for pilgrims who walk in the footsteps of Francis and Clare. It is very simple: a reading, a hymn, and tracing on the forehead with oil a simple sign of the cross, just as St. Clare healed others by tracing the sign of the cross over them.

I have seen many tears in Clare's dormitory, have witnessed healings of heart and mind, and have heard from fellow pilgrims how they found peace there in surrendering to God's will. One pilgrim a few years ago, a non-Catholic with a fervent piety and reverence for the saints, was suffering from what he did not know at the time was cancer of the esophagus. In St. Clare's dormitory he experienced a deep peace in the healing ritual, and one year later, on the Feast of St. Clare, he entered heaven without fear of dying, wholly resigned to God's will. Peace of heart was Clare's gift of healing to him.

So it is that year after year St. Clare's dormitory becomes a focal point of healing for pilgrims. St. Francis used to send others to Clare for healing, including Brother Stephen, one of his Brothers afflicted with an emotional/mental problem that caused seizures and screaming. Through the simple sign of the cross and directing Brother Stephen to sleep in the choir stall where she prayed, St. Clare became an instrument of healing for him. His seizures ceased and he returned to the Brothers healed.

Today eight hundred years later, we stand and draw the same sign of the cross on each other in Clare's dormitory. We trust in our own and each other's faith and on the intercession of St. Clare. What healing happens is God's work, not ours. As with the grace of pilgrimage itself, healing is something only God can effect. Ours is to make the pilgrimage, pray for healing, surrender to God's will.

Tangible results may or may not be immediately evident, but something always happens, something we may not be aware of until months afterwards.

Some find themselves making life-changing decisions within a year of returning from pilgrimage, and they realize their decisions were the result of walking in the footsteps of St. Francis and St. Clare.

Such decisions, in turn, may be the healing we were seeking along the way. We were waiting for something to happen to us, for God to intervene in our lives, when what was needed was really for us to make a decision that would change our own situation, making it possible for peace and wholeness to begin to root. The very non-effect of a pilgrimage we so anticipated can be the point of illumination for us. We need to do something, make a decision, act, and then the grace of pilgrimage will be ours.

We realize that God does not force our wills. God created us with a will free to choose; once we do choose to change what is debilitating and destructive, the healing begins. The change might not happen all of a sudden, but the healing has begun. Then little by little with successive decisions toward health and holiness, we begin to change.

We thought, perhaps, that the pilgrimage would effect an immediate healing, a dramatic change; we learn instead that healing and wholeness come slowly as we respond to God's grace, making decisions big and small that counter darkness and negativity, destructive behavior and sin. Acts of virtue negate sin; acts of adoration and thanksgiving negate those negative moods and the attitudes which before had led us to see everything as bleak, doomed, and unfulfilling.

At San Damiano St. Francis sang his greatest song of praise, "The Canticle of the Creatures." He had recently returned from La Verna, the mountain where a few weeks before he had received the sacred stigmata. He was legally blind from an eye disease probably contracted in Egypt when he journeyed there to try and bring peace between Crusaders and Muslims on the Fifth Crusade.

He was suffering from malnutrition and what was probably a tubercular form of leprosy. He was discouraged by what he perceived as his brothers' departure from their original commitment to gospel poverty. So he went not to his brothers at St. Mary of the Angels, but to San Damiano where Clare and the Poor Ladies had a small hut built beside the monastery. There Francis could rest and pray.

He lay there in darkness—the sun would cause his eyes to hemorrhage—for over fifty days with field mice running over his body. Then in a vision God showed him the earth renewed and asked him if his suffering would have been worthwhile if in exchange he would receive a treasure so great that if the whole earth were turned to gold, it would be as nothing compared to that treasure?

Francis said, "Oh yes, Lord, it would." God said, "Then be happy because I assure you that one day you will enjoy the Kingdom of Heaven—it is as certain as if you were already there."

Francis then responded by singing his great "Canticle of the Creatures":

> Most High, all-powerful, good Lord.
> Yours is the praise, the glory, and the honor,
> And every blessing.
> They belong to you alone, Most High,
> And no one is worthy to speak your name.
>
> So, praised be you, my Lord, with all your creatures,
> Especially Sir Brother Sun
> Who makes the day and enlightens us through you.

He is lovely and radiant and grand;
And he heralds you, his Most High Lord.

Praised be you, my Lord, through Sister Moon
And the stars.
You have hung them in heaven shining and precious
    and fair.

And praise to you, My Lord, through Brother Wind.
Through air and cloud, calm, and every weather
That sustains your creatures.

Praised be you, my Lord, through Brother Fire.
Through him you illumine our night,
And he is handsome and merry, robust and strong.

Praised be you, my Lord, through our Sister
Mother Earth,
Who nourishes us and teaches us,
Bringing forth all kinds of fruits and colored flowers
    and herbs.

Praise to you, my Lord,
Through those who forgive one another in your love
And who bear sickness and trials.
Blessed are they who live on in peace,
For they will be crowned by you, Most High.

Praise to you, my Lord, through our Sister Bodily Death,
From whom no one living can escape.
How dreadful for those who die in sin,
How lovely for those who are found in your
Most Holy Will,
For the second death can do them no harm.

O praise and bless my Lord,
Thank him and serve him
Humbly but grandly!

It was two years before his death that Francis sang his Canticle. His joy is evidence enough for us that Francis had made those decisions in his life—hard as they seemed at the time and in their fulfilling—that transformed a spoiled merchant's son into a poor beggar filled with joy in his love of Christ, whose love moved Francis to follow in his footsteps. Each decision for Christ along the way had little by little healed Francis and made him into a man who embraced with joy all of God's creation, lifting it up to the source of its very being, the good God whose face is revealed in Jesus Christ.

Francis, like us, became a pilgrim whose decisions along the way worked the transformation and grace he went seeking for, as the gift of reaching his destination. The destination beckons, inspires; the decisions along the way work the transformation that is the destination.

So it was with us who came in the staggering June heat. We chose to come to San Damiano to Clare's dormitory. We found that the burning sun was indeed our brother, because our hope was renewed though the heat was oppressive and the room barren of any furniture to sit upon. We stood or sat on the floor. We were physically uncomfortable.

But as we received the sign of the cross at the hands of a fellow pilgrim, the heat seemed insignificant to the warmth of the holy oil on our forehead. The less than comfortable surroundings made the comfort of the body seem insignificant to the consolation of mind and heart and soul.

Something had happened inside, some purification, some measure of healing, a renewed faith. We decided to come, even in the heat of the day. We were transformed by outer and inner sun, our Brother, who heralds the Most High Lord.

❋ The Basilica of St. Francis

A t any moment of our life, where we are is where we've come from. Our arrival is our departure and the way of arriving.

It is 1937, St. Mary's Hospital, Gallup, New Mexico, 10:30 PM. A Franciscan Sister is holding a newborn baby boy, lifting him up to the tranquil arms of Mary, the Mother of Jesus, offering this boy whose difficult birth by Caesarean section has marked him and his mother. They are both blessed with life, though the passage has been fraught with danger.

It is July, 2003, Assisi, Italy. That same boy kneels before the statue of Mary in the Lady Chapel in the lower Basilica of St. Francis. He offers his sixty-six years to her, marked with blessings, though the passage from boy to man has had the usual difficulties, and the intervening places along the way were quite other than what he had expected. The places and people the boy had to leave and those he met along the way have stamped his heart with the kind of prayers he offers and how he talks to her into whose care an anonymous Franciscan Sister offered the newborn boy. He is the story of his arrival here.

It is the story of every person now in this Basilica, including St. Francis, and his companions buried here near his tomb. Who we are is how and where we've traveled.

It may have been our own country we traveled, or even our own town. Such is not the boy's case, nor that of the other pilgrims here with me in Assisi. Ours has been a journey away from our own towns towards lands and sites previously known only from TV or movies or Lives of the Saints whose tombs we visit here, trying to touch the spirits of those whom God touched and who in turn have touched our lives.

Our pilgrimage to these shrines is a homage to, and thanksgiving for, the gift of their lives. We are transformed or enlightened or simply different because of these saints and personages, and we hope that through the journey and when we arrive they will communicate something further to us.

Here in the Basilica are buried St. Francis and four of his early companions, Brothers Leo, Ruffino, Angelo and Masseo. At the entrance of the crypt is buried Lady Jacoba dei Settesoli, a rich Roman woman who befriended St. Francis and whom Francis named Brother Jacoba for her love of the poor and her devotion to Francis and the early Brothers.

Here in this holy place of the remains, the relics of St. Francis, his life, too, came back to where it began. His relics lie surrounded by one of the greatest churches and art repositories of the Middle Ages. Here the great artists of the time came to do homage to the Little Poor Man of Assisi: Cimabue, Giotto, Lorenzetti, and Martini. He who was totally poor, who rejected the world of wealth and power, is feted with a place of inestimable wealth and spiritual power. He who gave up the possession of things, is surrounded by a thing of beauty. Where he is, is where he came from.

Here in this Basilica the reward of the poor gospel life is depicted. The Basilica is the tangible expression in stone and art of Francis' position in heaven, his reward. The riches of heaven and the riches of people on earth are lavished upon him. He who was once a rich young man has, by the way of poverty and renunciation, become again the rich man of the Kingdom of God.

Here beneath this Basilica lies what once was called, "Colle dell' Inferno," Hill of Hell, because criminals were executed here. There is a legend which says that the dying Francis asked to be buried in the most despised spot in Assisi. It came to pass. He was buried on the Hill of Hell, outside the walls of Assisi, and in so doing, transformed this hellish place into a Hill of Paradise where pilgrims come to do homage and ask for favors, where the very walls of the Upper and Lower churches of this huge structure are covered with some of the greatest frescoes in the history of art.

There is a story that Francis's mother once said to her neighbors who were gossiping about her son's extravagance:"You'll see what my son will be. Through grace, he will become a son of God." It has come to pass. Francis is venerated here as a true son of God, poor in this world's goods, rich in grace and clothed once again, as he was as a boy, with rich garments, the garments of virtue and glory so beautifully depicted in Giotto's allegorical frescoes in the Lower Basilica.

Where we are is where we've come from, transformed by the way of arriving.

❋ La Verna

Rome is hot; La Verna is cool. Rome is dry; La Verna is wet—its damp caves soggy with moisture in summer, frigid with ice in winter.

St. Francis loved the mountains, the Tuscan mountain of La Verna, especially, with its lush wet woods of beech, pine, and fir. He would enter the dark caves as into the womb of God to pray there intimately with Jesus, who lay inside the earth for three days before rising to the new life he promised us.

Francis was that literal, that concrete in his imitation of Christ, or as he would put it, in his following in the footsteps of Christ. To enter the earth was to enter the tomb with Christ; to emerge was to celebrate the Resurrection; to descend the mountain and to walk the roads barefoot was to witness to the gospel. Thus, each journey up the mountain, into the cave and down the mountain again, was a mini-pilgrimage that mirrored all the pilgrimages of Francis's life: from Assisi to St. Mary of the Angels, three miles below on the plain where the lepers lived; from St. Mary of the Angels to the Rieti Valley; from the Rieti Valley to Rome and back again to Assisi; from Assisi to much of Italy; to

Dalmatia, Syria and Egypt. Like his Lord and Savior, he walked as a pilgrim and stranger in this world with no place to call his own. Wherever he was, he sought out places of solitude and silence as here at La Verna, about a hundred miles north of Assisi.

Here on pilgrimage, I seek the same solitude and silence on this sunlit day in June. I am sitting in the small, cave-like chapel of St. Bonaventure located below the main chapel that marks the spot where St. Francis received the five wounds of Christ, the sacred stigmata so often celebrated in art. In this tiny chapel St. Bonaventure prayed and wrote his *Itinerarium Mentis in Deum, The Journey of the Person to God,* a spiritual classic of the Middle Ages. I've come here to pray because of my affinity with and devotion to St. Bonaventure.

St. Bonaventure was a theologian, a Doctor of the Church, and Minister General of the Franciscan Order, who even in the midst of his administrative and fraternal duties as Minister General of the friars and later as a Cardinal, still found time (or made time) to write. I've come here to ask him to help me find words for what happened on this mountain in September of 1224, and these are the words that flow from my pen:

"Here is where Love was loved, here is where Francis was betrothed to Christ in a profound mystical marriage of souls. Francis becomes outwardly what he has been inwardly for most of his adult life: an ecstatic lover of the crucified Christ. From the moment when, as a young man of twenty, Francis heard the voice of the crucified Christ speak to him from the San Damiano crucifix, it is to Christ crucified that he relates most intimately.

"It is this same crucified Christ that St. Francis meets in the person of a leper on the road below Assisi.

He gives alms to the leper and embraces him, and when Francis remounts his horse and turns to wave, the leper has vanished. Francis knows he has embraced Christ, the poor crucified Savior, and he leaves his riches, his family, his home town of Assisi, and descends the steep incline of the spur of Mount Subasio where Assisi rests like a shimmering stone-red fortress and lives on the swampy plain below with the poor "Christs," the lepers who've been excluded from the town above.

"In so doing, Francis experiences deep sweetness of soul. What before was bitter to him, as he writes in his Testament, was now turned into sweetness of soul.

"Thus it was that more than twenty years later when he makes his final ascent of Mount La Verna, he has already been crucified with Christ. The stigmata is but the external sign of the wounded heart St. Francis already is. But the sacred stigmata is more. It confirms for Francis and for us that holiness is not something wholly of the soul. Holiness is wholeness; it's about the whole person, body and soul. Holiness is the incarnation in the body of the true face of the soul in union with God. Holiness is the truth of who we are: one person, whole and entire, and not a dichotomy of body and soul, or worse, of body versus soul.

"The stigmata of St. Francis reminds us powerfully and visually of the centrality of the Incarnation in Christian spirituality. Because of the Incarnation of God in Jesus Christ, we know that our bodies are good and holy and are not to be relegated to some inferior prison house for the soul. We know that just as Jesus rose from the dead, body and soul, so shall we rise in the end time when Christ returns to claim as his own all of creation.

"Just as God is Three Persons, yet one God, so are we body, soul, and spirit, yet one person. We are body;

we are the soul that gives life to the body; we are Spirit of God dwelling in us; and yet we are one person, a mirror image of the Trinitarian God in whose image we are made. This great mystery is made visual for us in the sacred stigmata, which St. Francis received on Mt. La Verna."

These words came all in a rush as I sat in the chapel of St. Bonaventure and are dense with theology because they contain the theological implications of the stigmata of St. Francis. What happened in St. Francis's body on La Verna was the mirror of what had already happened in his soul. He had been crucified with Christ through penance and deprivation and taking up his cross daily in the footsteps of his Savior.

The sacred stigmata also attests to the unity of body and soul, to one person, not a person divided into body and soul, or a person with a good soul trapped in a bad body. St. Francis is outwardly who he is inwardly. La Verna marked the crucifixion of Francis. When he died two years later, the Porziuncola, the little church on the plain below Assisi, marked his rising.

All this theology came to me as I sat praying in the chapel of the Franciscan Order's great theologian, St. Bonaventure. Bonaventure's was the language of theology, and theological language was what I was given as a pilgrim turning to him for guidance on how to write about the mystery of St. Francis's stigmata.

Who the saints were they are now. They give us now what they gave to others when they lived on earth. We are in heaven who we were on earth. Francis is not Bonaventure, nor Bonaventure Francis. One is a theologian, the other a troubadour and poet; one gives us a cathedral of words, the other a simple poem made of the gestures of his life, like the miracle that took place here.

What encouragement and what peace this affords us as pilgrims. We are who we uniquely are—a truth revealed to us more deeply on our spiritual quest.

❋ Mary, the Pilgrim

Pilgrims to Assisi are drawn to the plain below the town, to the Porziuncola (Little Portion), a tiny chapel inside the present Basilica of St. Mary of the Angels. At the beginning, when Francis and his first Brothers were but twelve in number, they lived first in an old abandoned shed at Rivo Torto, not far from the Porziuncola. These accommodations quickly proved inadequate, and through the Bishop of Assisi Francis obtained from the Benedictine Monks of Mount Subasio the use of the Porziuncola, for which he paid a yearly basket of fish.

Francis restored the Porziuncola with his own hands, and it became the center of Francis's movement. Francis and the Brothers lived in small huts around the chapel. From there they ministered to the lepers who lived in colonies on the surrounding plain; there Francis received St. Clare into the Order; there Francis had a vision that led him to ask for and receive from Pope Honorius III a plenary indulgence for all of those who visit this small chapel and pray for the intentions of the Holy Father; and there Francis died on October 3, 1226.

Francis loved this chapel because it was dedicated to Mary, Queen of the Angels. A fourteenth century painting by Ilario da Viterbo over the altar of the Porziuncola chapel depicts the Annunciation to Mary by the angel Gabriel.

In the summer of 2003 I sat contemplating the painting and meditating in the Franciscan way I was taught almost fifty years before as a young novice and that has sustained me over the years. It is sometimes called "The Mysticism of the Historical Event" and consists of taking a passage or scene from sacred Scripture and imagining it as vividly as possible. Placing oneself in the scene and letting the events that unfold reveal their spiritual power can move you to live out in your daily life the lessons you draw from participating imaginatively in the scene. It is how I pray on pilgrimage, often surprised and grateful for the graces of this kind of meditation.

I have made many pilgrimages to the Porziuncola, but always my meditations were on how Francis founded his Order here and how Francis and his Brothers ministered to the lepers. This time was different. Mary, Our Lady of the Angels, emerged.

Sitting in the chapel looking at the painting of the angel Gabriel, I began to meditate on the scene, and Mary emerged as an image of the pilgrim soul.

She's at home in Nazareth. Praying in her room? Carding wool? Staring out the window thinking about her future, dreaming young girls' dreams or simply moving about her room, thinking nothing in particular?

Whatever she's doing, suddenly there's a rush of angel wings and a voice pure, and trembling with the movement of wings now settling, folding inward. It is Gabriel, Archangel, God's messenger. Mary is about to move beyond her world: her parents' home, her town, her own personal space of being.

'Greetings, favored one! The Lord is with you' (Lk. 1:28).

Out of what anonymity and littleness is she being called! This young girl, all of fourteen years old. Who is she that an angel should visit her, descend to Nazareth, a remote city in the vast Roman Empire, and say to her that the Lord is with her? How astonishing and terrifying that greeting must sound in her ears, her soul!

She is not dreaming; for shaking herself and looking about the room, everything is as it's always been, except that he's still there, the angel, kneeling now and saying further, in a rush of words like sparks fanned by his powerful wings, 'Do not be afraid, Mary for you have found favor with God. And now, you will conceive in your womb and bear a son, and you will name him Jesus. He will be great, and will be called the Son of the Most High, and the Lord God will give to him the throne of his ancestor David. He will reign over the house of Jacob forever, and of his kingdom there will be no end' (Lk. 1:30–33).

The words. They echo the sounds and cadences of the prophets, they remind her of what she'd thought of and prayed over as she rehearsed the words of Isaiah in her prayer: "Look, the young woman is with child and shall bear a son, and shall name him Immanuel" (Is. 7:14). And again, "For a child has been born for us, a son given to us; authority rests upon his shoulders; and he is named Wonderful, Counselor, Mighty God, Everlasting Father, Prince of Peace" (Is. 9:6).

Isn't Joseph, her betrothed, of the house of David? And yes, she was afraid before this angelic presence, one of those powerful ministering spirits who surround God's throne, his voice filling the silence; his resonance deep and rich with the music of eternity.

What is he saying; what is he calling her to, this manlike creature who's invaded her space? She will conceive and bear a son? Will this messenger himself be the father? What is happening? But he has said, "Fear not," and so she will not fear but simply ask, 'How can this be, since I am a virgin?' (Lk. 1:34).

Indeed, how can this be? Will this messenger tell her? What is she being called to? Can it be she he is talking to now as he says, 'The Holy Spirit will come upon you, and the power of the Most High will overshadow you; therefore the child to be born will be holy; he will be called Son of God. And now, your relative Elizabeth in her old age has also conceived a son; and this is the sixth month for her who was said to be barren. For nothing will be impossible with God' (Lk. 1:35–39).

Who is this Holy Spirit? What does "overshadow" mean? The air is pregnant with silence. She can refuse; even in her youth, she knows this. Perhaps she should, or is there no response expected of her? The angel seems to be waiting for a response, yet she doesn't feel forced. She intuitively knows that it is up to her to say yes; this Holy Spirit will do the rest.

She thinks. She sees Elizabeth, that holy woman, her cousin, who now, the angel says, is six months with child, for nothing is impossible with God. Already she feels the powerful yet soft overshadowing of the Holy Spirit which the angel spoke of. This Spirit feels familiar, she knows this presence, it is rising from within her and now hovers above her, and she says almost in a hushed whisper, 'Here am I, the servant of the Lord; let it be with me according to your word' (Lk 1:38).

Whether to the angel or to the Holy Spirit, or both, she has said it. She is now being led by that same Spirit beyond her familiar world into a world that will be. She has become a pilgrim, one whose whole life will be faith in the unfolding of God's promise; and everything now will not be what it seems. It will be more: a sign, a symbol, a reality that contains a deeper, other reality that is its meaning, its purpose, its destination.

All she needs to do is listen and respond and store up memories in her heart. For there are angels about and there is the Holy Spirit, who has come upon her, freeing her from the bondage of herself and simultaneously making her totally herself. The power of the Most High God now overshadows her and she is wholly God's servant, yet wholly herself.

Thus begins Mary's pilgrim way. Wholly rapt in God, she does not rest there. Not hoarding her treasure for herself, for her own sweet contemplation; she immediately thinks of Elizabeth and rushes—her first pilgrimage—to a town in the hill country of Judea where she enters Zechariah's home and greets Elizabeth. At Mary's greeting the baby in Elizabeth's womb leaps for joy, and she, too, is filled with the Spirit and cries out, 'Blessed are you among women, and blessed is the fruit of your womb. And why has this happened to me, that the mother of my Lord comes to me? For as soon as I heard the sound of your greeting, the child in my womb leaped for joy. And blessed is she who believed that there would be a fulfillment of what was spoken to her by the Lord' (Lk. 1:42–45).

Mary, hearing these words, knows there's someone else who understands, someone she can talk to, someone to share what no one else could take in. Perhaps she knew that as soon as the angel spoke to her of Elizabeth, perhaps that was part of her eagerness to visit Elizabeth, not only to console and help her, but to be near a kindred soul, an older woman who would help her seem less alone with her secret. And so, hearing Elizabeth's words, which Mary knows instinctively are coming from the same Holy Spirit that has come upon her, she breaks into song, a poem of praise whose words are coming from Mary but also from the ages before her. She is singing her song that is simultaneously the prophets' song, the Jewish people's song of longing. Already a double reality is happening, the reality of a song that is hers yet more: a symbol, a sign, of something within all of history, an echo of the eternal plan of God.

> My soul magnifies the Lord,
>   and my spirit rejoices in God my Savior,
> for he has looked with favor
>   on the lowliness of his servant.
> Surely, from now on all generations
>   will call me blessed;
>   for the Mighty One has done great things for me,
>   and holy is his name.
> His mercy is for those who fear him
>   from generation to generation.
> He has shown strength with his arm;
>   he has scattered the proud in the thoughts
>   of their hearts.
> He has brought down the powerful
>   from their thrones, and lifted up the lowly;
> he has filled the hungry with good things,
>   and sent the rich away empty.
> He has helped his servant Israel,
>   in remembrance of his mercy,
> according to the promise he made
>   to our ancestors,
>   to Abraham and his descendants forever (Lk 1:46–55).

Her soul, small and insignificant before God, makes God big, magnifies God for those whose vision is weak; for those for whom God has become too small to see because of their own self-inflation or because of their weak faith, their sin, their absorption in this world, in themselves alone; for those, in short, upon whom the Holy Spirit has not yet come as it will through her and Elizabeth and the two children they bear in their wombs.

It is all beginning, the fulfillment of the promises, the coming of the Messiah. And yes, who is Elizabeth that the mother of her Lord should come to her, and who is she, Mary, that the Holy Spirit should come upon her and the power of the Most High should be magnified in her? It is a mystery. She will store up Elizabeth's words in her heart; she will remember everything Elizabeth says during her three-month sojourn with her; she will continue to listen, continue to believe though she does not and will not understand fully what is happening.

She will remain a woman from Nazareth; whatever else radiates from her will be of the child within and of the Holy Spirit who is both child and progenitor of the child. In the meantime she will live in the ordinary world of women in pregnancy, of poverty, of life with Joseph, of all the ordinary menial details of life which now are suffused with something other which will break forth both to her joy and to her sorrow as she brings forth her child, nourishes him, follows him on his way back to where he came from in the Holy Spirit's enveloping her.

How hard it will be at times to hold on to the memories she has stored up in her heart, how hard to hold on to the reality within the reality. That becomes evident already in the child's birthing which takes place on her second pilgrimage from Nazareth in Galilee to Judea to Bethlehem, the town of David. She goes with Joseph to register with him whom she is pledged to marry though she is already with child. They go seemingly in obedience to Caesar Augustus, the Roman Emperor who has ordered a census of the whole Roman world.

And so it happens, though Mary still holds in her heart the reality of that other world operating within the world we can see with our human eyes. This is more than a journey to register their names, their existence, before the powerful Caesar and his representatives. Indeed it comes to pass that while they are in Bethlehem, she gives birth to her son and wraps him in swaddling clothes and places him in the manger of the stable where he is born because there was no room for them in the inn.

Like all pilgrims before and after her, Mary gives birth on the road, on the way, away from home. And though this little family seems alone, except for the animals, suddenly there are angels. Mary knows that once again the other world of the Spirit has broken through. Mary of the Angels—they've surrounded her child where they've been all along, hidden beneath the veil that separates them from human eyes. Once again, as with Gabriel, they come with a message—first to poor shepherds and through them to Mary and Joseph and all the people: 'Do not be afraid, for see—I am bringing you good news of great joy for all the people: to you is born this day in the city of David a Savior, who is the Messiah, the Lord. This will be a sign for you: you will find a child wrapped in bands of cloth and lying in a manger' (Lk. 2:10–12).

Mary knows that her son will begin with the poor, those whom this world sees as insignificant, those living in the hills tending sheep. Once again the sign, the symbol: shepherd, sheep, remote hillsides of the world— all, surrounded by angels. It is the world of the pilgrim, the side roads and byways of the way to God. Mary again treasures up all these things and ponders them in her heart: the strangers they meet on the way, the strangers who somehow find them and come to them, like the Magi, who follow their own star, their own way to him whom they say is born king of the Jews and whom they've come to worship.

Again something more is breaking through when they arrive, these non-Jews who enter unannounced, as Gabriel had, bowing down, worshiping her child, opening the treasures they've guarded so carefully: gold, incense and myrrh, thinking he is a king of another kind for whom gold and precious ointments are due. How could they know his kingdom was not of this world, though gold and precious stones and rich treasures would one day adorn his temples? Nor did she see that yet; she only saw these strange men who somehow knew her son was to be adored, whose pilgrimage to him had been long and hard and whose peoples would not have understood, would not have approved their following a star that led them away from their own culture, their own way.

But Mary understood as soon as they bowed down, understood in the Spirit, as Elizabeth had when Mary entered her home, that the same Spirit had overshadowed these wise men from the East. Her pilgrimage with Joseph to Bethlehem, the city of David, now intersected with another pilgrimage, a pilgrimage of those who watch and study the heavens for signs of something more happening on earth than we are normally aware of.

Like pilgrims of all times, Mary has experienced much on the road, away from home, knowing the Holy Spirit will and is made manifest when we are simply doing what life and duty and love demand of us. What was first revealed to her at home and drew her out of the tight confines of Nazareth to Elizabeth's home in the hill country of Judea, will continue to call her forth and be revealed on the road away from home, revealed even through those who are strangers and unlikely messengers of the Spirit. A family of believers is beginning to happen even outside the Jewish people.

I pause and look up at the painting of the Annunciation here in this tiny chapel, and I think of Francis and how he too began to experience a new family outside the walls of Assisi; how he heard the voice of Christ from the San Damiano crucifix outside the walls of his home town; how he met the leper on the road below the city and realized in embracing the leper that he was embracing Christ; how he went to live among the lepers, and there others joined him and a new family in Christ began to grow among the outcasts and neglected of society; how he walked the roads of Italy and beyond, as far as Damietta in Egypt where he met the Sultan and listened to him and the two talked of God and the Sultan gave Francis safe passage to walk the roads of his kingdom; how so much of Francis's life and Francis's encounters with God happened on the road.

I, too, rise from my place in this chapel and take to the road again, inspired by Mary and Francis to believe that the pilgrim way does indeed bring us to God. I begin the journey home, which is itself full of possibilities for encounter with the Christ who himself walked the roads of this world.

So I leave the Little Portion and walk through the vast Basilica that shelters this small chapel. I walk out into the sunlit piazza in front of the Basilica. I bow to the statue of Mary atop the high façade and walk to the train station. I look up to the distant city of Assisi gleaming white and pink in the noonday sun as I wait for the train that will speed me away for another year. I look back at the dome of the Basilica and pray,

"Mary, Our Lady of the Angels, guide us on our way, be our own dear mother on this and our final pilgrimage."

✳ *Coming Home*

Coming home. How beautiful is the landscape of home after an extended absence, after crossing the long field that is pilgrimage. One of the roots of the word, *pilgrim*, is to go through a field. No matter how drawn we are to make that crossing—to find the blessings inviting us to shrines and holy places beyond, it is home that is made more beautiful and full of grace when we return.

The poet T.S. Eliot says it best in these lines from "Little Gidding:"

> We shall not cease from exploration
> and the end of all our exploring
> will be to arrive where we started
> and know the place for the first time.[xiv]

As moving as it was to see the Statue of Liberty recede on the horizon as we sailed out of New York, it could not compare to the first view of the statue as we reentered New York harbor. The faults of America not withstanding, that awesome sight is the first glimmering of home and the loved ones waiting for our return.

I thought, as we drew near, about the word *return* and how that is exactly what coming home is. We turned away to seek God where we perceived God's call was beckoning us. And having responded and made the journey of soul and body, we turn again and re-trace our steps back to the door from which we left.

That word *turn* is weighted with meaning for Christians because it is rooted in overtones of conversion. The Greek word, *metanoia,* means to turn about, a *conversio,* a turning around, and that is what we have learned on the pilgrim way. We turn toward God, and we thereby re-turn to where we came from. Turning to God turns us back upon our roots—our origins in the God we somehow lost or became alienated from or grew indifferent to. By turning toward God's beckoning call, we re-found how good and beautiful we are in being created by God, being born into a given landscape and blessed with life for as many years as our pilgrimage on earth will last. We know, too, that just as we turned to God and re-turned toward home, so in the end we will turn again to God and find ourselves returning forever to our true home which is God.

Even if *home* conjures up negative or violent images of a destructive childhood, the journey away on pilgrimage to and with God, gradually heals our broken past and redeems the time we thought was irrevocably lost. "All things work together for good for those who love God," St. Paul says (Ro. 8:28a). That is true even of the past, which the more we walk with God, becomes just that—the past—and we are now in the present, made new, having turned to God and thereby re-turned to our true home.

This turning and re-turning is not easy. It involves forgiving our past and those who ruined it for us; those who hurt us. It involves forgiving ourselves that we are broken or somehow ugly in our own eyes. It involves forgiving God for letting it all happen. On that long road to forgiving, the world is made beautiful again, and we come to see that nothing is unchangeable, that God can turn even brokenness and sin into grace and virtue and wholeness.

Perhaps this is one reason why the place we call home seems so fresh and new when we re-turn. We have been transformed; we have returned to childhood and we see again with a bit of the innocence of the child. Jesus says, 'Whoever does not receive the kingdom of God as a little child will never enter it.' (Lk. 18:17). That, too, is an effect of the pilgrim way: it helps us see that the Kingdom of heaven is all around us and within us. We have already entered it when we responded to God's call and set forth (on an actual geographical journey or a journey into the heart) wholly dependent on God, with a child's trust in a loving parent who shows us how beautiful is the world within and without.

St. Bonaventure says that justice means making beautiful that which has been deformed. Perhaps that is what walking the pilgrim way is also about: making justice, making beautiful that which we all know has been deformed by human sin and failure. Ultimately it is a return to the Garden of Eden by way of the way of the Cross; it is our personal walking through the history of salvation as it was made concrete for us in the life of Christ, who sums up all of human history in his birth, life, death, and resurrection. In the words of St. Paul,

> He is the image of the invisible God, the firstborn of all
> creation; for in him all things in heaven and on earth were
> created, things visible and invisible, whether thrones or
> dominions or rulers or powers—all things have been created
> through him and for him. He himself is before all things,

and in him all things hold together. . . . For in him all the fullness of God was pleased to dwell, and through him God was pleased to reconcile to himself all things, whether on earth or in heaven, by making peace through the blood of his cross (Col. 1:15–17, 19-20).

What a journey Paul must have made to write those words; what a journey we must make to believe them and see for ourselves!

All pilgrimage, whether into the heart or across the landscape, or both, are ultimately journeys home, a home transformed into its original innocence by our walking in the footsteps of him, who is again 'making all things new' (Rev. 21:5).

PART THREE
Meditations on Returning Home

Sometimes we go on a search
and do not know what we are looking for,
until we come again to our beginning.
        Robert Lax

❋ 1.

To be on pilgrimage is to be away from home, whatever that means to each of us. For one it may be welcome relief from a stifling environment; for another a long anticipated adventure; for another an anxiety about change. Whatever the feelings attendant upon being away from home, sooner or later there is homesickness, that longing to return, that feeling of being displaced and set down among strangers whose ways are not our own.

As pilgrims we become painfully aware that on some level we have become dependent on the mercy and kindness of others. Those others may or may not be welcoming. Along the way pilgrims are forced to relate to all types of people and become aware of the whole spectrum of humanity. To be pilgrims is to go among others not of our own choosing who themselves are pilgrims on this earth, but who may have the illusory power of place with which to lord it over those who have no place of their own—for a time or even permanently.

The pilgrim, then, becomes a sign to others of their own mortality and the transience of their seeming power over their lives. For those who can see and whose hearts are open, the pilgrim reminds them of the instability of their own lives, of the passing nature of all things. It is the pilgrim who feels uprootedness, instability and alienation most poignantly. Where are my friends the pilgrim asks? How is my family doing? What is happening back home? Who is caring for my loved ones? Why did I ever set out on this journey in the first place? What have I been able to bring with me from home?

The last question, particularly, leads the pilgrim inward, and slowly the pilgrim realizes: I am aware of memory and love and my very self as a portable home that makes present to me everything I left behind. I am beginning to re-evaluate, or perhaps value properly for the first time, what home means. Gradually, I've begun to see home as a grander, more permanent reality than the place I call my home. Home becomes both my final destination and my very self which will be my home in the home that is God.

God is home, but God is only seen clearly as our home in eternity. There we will see clearly that all along we have been joined to God as our origin and our end. In God we see fully the home that our own uniqueness is. In God we are wholly ourselves, for in God we find the one who created, redeemed, and sanctified us, making a home in us for all eternity—as God was home in us on our pilgrimage through life, though we only saw it vaguely as in a dream.

2.

We need not travel to a sacred shrine or be "on the road" to be a pilgrim. To be a pilgrim is also a psychological state in which we feel alienated or a stranger where we live. We feel "outside the loop" of where others are. Perhaps it is because our ideas or convictions are rejected by others and they make us feel apart from them, on the fringe of what the majority of our countrymen believe and commit themselves to. We may feel like a pilgrim and stranger because the values we hold dearly are belittled and rejected by those in power. As in actually making a pilgrimage, what is important is how we respond to this feeling of alienation and marginalization.

What keeps us going? What gives us faith and hope that we still matter even as a pilgrim, a sojourner? How do we bring charity, redeeming love, to those we meet along the way? Who are those who reach out to us in love and compassion? Ultimately, what really matters when all the trappings of belonging, of power and influence, are stripped away?

To be reduced to nothing is to have everything. When everything we wrongly thought would make us happy is stripped away, we are thrown back onto our own resources. We are forced to find that place within that is our true home, the place where God dwells, the very center of our unique self. This is our immortal soul, uniquely stamped with God's creative love. At this center we begin to be born again into a whole new way of being. We begin to live wholly dependent on the creative providence of God. In that dependence is the freedom Jesus promises in the first Beatitude:

'Blessed are the poor in spirit, for theirs is the kingdom of heaven' (Mt. 5:3).

In having the kingdom of heaven here, we have everything. To be reduced to nothing, then, is to have everything.

✳ 3.

In the Judeo-Christian tradition a pilgrim also connotes a sojourner, a temporary resident on this earth, and thereby signifies a special relationship to this world. Our true home being heaven, this world is seen in this tradition as the temporary sojourn of one on the way to heaven, one who is but an exile from one's true home as long as one dwells on this earth.

But that does not mean that we despise the world or reject it. On the contrary, in going on pilgrimage or in having a pilgrim heart, we see the world for the first time, the world we've been looking at all along. We haven't had the time, the leisure to see what is really around us. Going on pilgrimage forces us to see things we never noticed before, even the weather and the way the trees look. A day sitting in our chair watching television, the shades pulled down so there won't be a glare on the screen—a day like that could be a day on the road, a day of walking and looking, taking in the sights and sounds and smells, taking in the vibrations of the world around us. And even though we are still in the process of taking in, this experience is not as passive as sitting idly back and watching television. It is something more active; we are more engaged with our whole body. The crunch of autumn leaves under our feet; or the squeaking of boots in winter snow; or the smell of spring, of new flowers coming out, of fresh grass; or the lazy musty smell and feel of summer, deep summer, August days, engages us.

This dimension of pilgrimage, this new awareness, can also be a pilgrimage of memory, because as we walk along, as we look perhaps at the fall trees around us, their yellows, their oranges, their reds, we begin to remember days as a child when our father took us out fishing or hunting. It's been a long time since we've had the feelings we had then, the freshness of the world around us, the fact of being with our father. Or we remember going out with our mother shopping or perhaps even out into the fields walking through the fallen leaves, perhaps even playing with our mother; we wonder why we haven't done more of that. As we walk along, we begin to kick the piling leaves, bend over and gather up an armful of leaves and throw them up into the air. We begin to feel like a child again. We try to remember the magic of the world of our childhood, the things we played with, the friends we had. Where are they are now, do they have children and grandchildren?

At present I'm making a pilgrimage by car. I look at the autumn trees around me. It's November and yet the trees are still freshly yellow and red. I'm traveling just outside Washington, Pennsylvania, on my way to New Stanton, and I remember riding in the car with my father, how he would sing songs to me and tell me stories, how yesterday was his birthday, and he would be eighty-eight. I begin to remember the power of the spirit. I begin to feel again the power of his spirit.

✳ 4.

The Christian pilgrim takes consolation and strength from the words of Jesus, who said, 'Take nothing for their journey except a staff; no bread, no bag, no money in their belts. . . .' (Mk. 6:8). The pilgrim's prayer is Psalm 84:

> My soul longs, indeed it faints
> for the courts of the Lord;
> my heart and my flesh sing for joy
> to the living God.
> Happy those whose strength is in you,
> in whose heart are the highways to Zion.
> As they go through the valley of Baca
> they make it a place of springs;
> the early rain also covers it with pools.
> They go from strength to strength;
> the God of gods will be seen in Zion.
> For a day in your courts is better
> than a thousand elsewhere.
> For the Lord God is a sun and shield;
> he bestows favor and honor.
> No good thing does the Lord withhold
> from those who walk uprightly. (vv. 2, 5–7, 10a-11)

The Christian pilgrim goes forward with confidence and faith in the footsteps of the Lord, the savior Jesus Christ, who says to the pilgrim, "Come, follow me" (Mk. 10:21a). A vivid example of pilgrimage is the response of Jesus' Apostles, who went when Jesus called, "left their nets and followed him" (Mt. 4:20).

5.

To be purified, to atone for sins—this, too, is in the pilgrim's heart, making pilgrimage, at times, an examination of conscience, a time of penance. Where have I strayed? Where have I lost the way? Where did I choose not to follow the way? How can I get back on the right path again?

Going on pilgrimage is the beginning of a prolonged metaphor for starting over and walking again the path to God. The pilgrim reasons, if I can persevere on this relatively short journey, then maybe I can persevere on life's pilgrimage to God, as well. As with life itself, I cannot think of the entire journey; it is too overwhelming. So I think only of the day's journey, of getting from point A to point B in one day, persevering in God's grace as I make the journey from the rising of the sun to its setting.

The pilgrim knows there will be obstacles—obstacles from the pilgrim's own heart or obstacles from evil that has nothing to do with the pilgrim. For evil is jealous of good. In the Judeo-Christian tradition Satan/Lucifer, the fallen Angel, personifies an almost palpable force who is in rivalry with God for dominance over human souls.

This struggle between good and evil, more than anything else, makes us see we are but pilgrims and strangers on this earth. Our personal or collective evil, the evil that comes out of the human heart is not so much what convinces us, but the evil that we have no control over, the evil that befalls us despite our good intentions, our basically good heart.

Nor is there any answer to this mystery, except the one God gave us: the Incarnation of God, the birth, life, suffering, death and resurrection of Jesus Christ. His life is *the* paradigm of the pilgrim, the way to walk through life. We follow in Christ's footsteps; we find our meaning in him who said, 'I am the way, and the truth, and the life' (Jn. 14:6a).

Life is intrinsically flawed by some primeval touch of evil that God does not simply eradicate because it has something to do with us or our ancestors: a choice they made that only choice can redeem. So God chooses to redeem that human choice by becoming human and choosing to embrace God even in the face of terrible evil, the evil of betrayal and crucifixion that seems on the surface to show again that God is not ultimately there.

God seems to abandon his own Son, and Jesus dies on a cross. But then—and all our faith depends on this—God raises Jesus from the dead to become again what he always was, the eternal cosmic Christ, who sends us his Holy Spirit that we might overcome evil as he did by embracing Love, even when that Love seems not to be love as we know it, when Love has seemingly abandoned us to our own devices.

This is the lived faith of the pilgrim as he or she moves from point A to point B, whether that passage is a geographical journey or the journey of growing day by day in God's grace and love.

What an actual physical pilgrimage does is provide a metaphor, a circumscribed journey, that tests the human will and spirit the way that a liturgical season like Advent or Lent does. Both Advent and Lent are journeys of the spirit, one toward new birth, the other toward resurrection. Both involve a passage of purification and atonement whose goal is re-birth and resurrection. The pilgrim walks in penance, in other words, not thinking of the penance, but of the goal.

Such a walking in the footsteps of Christ is only possible if the Holy Spirit is given to us. That is why the pilgrim prepares for the journey ritually, for example, by partaking of the sacraments of penance and Eucharist. Only fortified in this way can the pilgrim embark on the journey which will itself be the atonement for one's sins in communion with Christ, who is *the* atonement for all sins.

Every tourist knows travel itself can be a penance. Even with first class tickets and accommodations, things happen. Flights are missed or canceled, luggage is lost; passports, purses and wallets are stolen; even hijackings and terrorist attacks can't be ruled out. But one doesn't concentrate on these negative possibilities; one thinks of the fun and adventure of travel and trusts that the trip will not be sabotaged.

The difference between the tourist and the pilgrim is in the response to these untoward happenings. For the tourist inconveniences and difficulties, illnesses and mishaps, ruin the trip and sometimes make the traveler swear off all future travel, especially to a country not one's own. For the pilgrim (already in a penitential attitude) such occurrences are viewed as part of the journey, as tests and trials, as obstacles to be overcome with faith and hope and love. The very journey itself has been begun in penance: the pilgrim travels lightly, unburdened by extra luggage, not traveling first class, as it were, but with the poor, in a spirit of spiritual poverty, dependent on God for whatever grace God will give along the way, grace that will be manifest in the people and events (both good and bad) that the pilgrim encounters.

Because the pilgrim is walking in the footsteps of Christ, there is even joy in difficulties and trials. There is joy in the knowledge that the pilgrim does not walk alone. Christ walks with and in me. But because I as pilgrim walk with Christ in goodness of heart, evil will be jealous and raise its head and try to keep me from persevering on and in the way. In that sense, then, pilgrimage is not without evil. The pilgrim knows that, but knows also that Christ has overcome evil. One has only to persevere in Christ's way, surrendering always to God's will, and all will be well; the pilgrimage will be completed, the transformation will happen on the way.

✳ 6.

Anyone who's gone on pilgrimage, or even the tourist knows how much more freely they travel who don't have a lot of baggage. The pilgrim knows that the small journey to a shrine, or to the holy places of one's religion, is a symbol of the journey home to God. The less baggage the better in order to remind the pilgrim of how little we take with us into eternity. Yet how much we take, as well, for we take with us our soul, the very center of who we are.

Material baggage can distract us from the soul, from the eternity we carry with us that is light and airy and immortal. Of all the symbolism of pilgrimage, this is the deepest, this sense of rehearsal for the soul-journey we are all making as we journey through this life to eternal life. It is a journey we hardly advert to when we are young, but which we become increasingly aware of as we age and move inextricably toward our final pilgrim goal, union with God.

As in all the movements of our lives, the smaller, daily passages we make, enable us to more easily make the great passages. Fasting, for example, reminds us that we do not live on bread alone, that there is another hunger that only spiritual food can satisfy. A journey with others to a holy shrine becomes an analog of the deeper, spiritual journey we have been making toward eternity; the larger journey, then, does not seem as daunting once we've seen that we can leave belongings, relatives and friends behind and focus on the spiritual, the soul-dimensions of our lives.

Going on pilgrimage necessarily requires a letting go; a surrender of power and control for the sake of a spiritual goal; an arrival that may or may not be a revelation, but that will bless our lives and renew our awareness of the deeper dimension of who we are, of what lies beneath the surface of life.

✳ 7.

The pilgrim often brings along an amulet of some kind, an icon, a photograph, a religious medal, a book. It becomes a focus, an anchor for the soul. Because I have been much on the road, I have felt the need again and again for an anchor, something to steady my soul, something to keep it from drifting. I have felt the need for a sense of place, of home, even as I move from place to place not my own. I reach for an anchor to steady me.

The anchor is small—a slim red book, its vinyl cover gold-embossed with a Celtic cross. It is a collection of morning and evening prayers from the Roman Breviary, the Book of Hours of the Church. I purchased this pocket-size volume years ago in Rome and have carried it with me ever since. I doubt if I would have bought it if it had been heavier, or a paperback. Its spine would be broken and its pages missing by now; the glued pages detached by heat and cold and use. But this little book has lasted. Its sewn Bible-paper pages are as secure as the Psalms and other Scripture readings it contains.

These pages soften and enlighten whatever space I am in. Even were I in prison, without this or any other book, the memory of holding this comforting volume and the gradually memorized words of its psalms, would, I hope, anchor my fear and loneliness.

A beautiful book—its texture, its tissue-like pages, the cadences of its canticles and psalms—often this is all I have had to anchor the frightening roll and pull of my unmoored soul. It has been sufficient.

✳ 8.

To be spiritual means that we are aware of a world within a world, a world of the Spirit that surrounds and is incarnate in the world we perceive with our senses. One way into that world is to go on pilgrimage, to walk real roads, to travel across the physical geography of earth, a journey that begins in the mind and imagination.

That, at least, is how spiritual pilgrimage began for me, both my first pilgrimage from New Mexico to Ohio and the later pilgrimages of my adult life.

I remember, as a teenager, on a bleak, sunless day I wouldn't look out the window. Instead, in the bright fluorescent library of the high school seminary, I'd look into books that didn't see the gray outdoors. Adventure books by Richard Halliburton and Thor Heyerdahl took me into the world the words made in my imagination. The places the words made were as far away as Tibet and the Pacific Polynesian Islands and as close as my own imagination taking me there. I was fourteen years old, a freshman, but I hoped somehow I would travel like Halliburton and Heyerdahl, not as an adventurer, but as a missionary.

I never became a foreign missionary, but I did travel to far-away places: England, Scotland, Ireland, France, the Netherlands, Germany, Switzerland, Spain, Greece, and above all, Italy. I became a pilgrim and a leader of pilgrims years after I sat enthralled by those adventure books on bleak Sunday afternoons.

These further pilgrimages began when I was teaching in the same seminary fourteen years later and was about to depart for Assisi for three months. I'd been given leave from teaching and spiritual direction of the seminarians from March to June, 1972. It was not the most propitious time for me. I was suffering from burnout.

Those brief three months became a pilgrimage of healing, of finding myself again. I re-found my Italian roots, and in the landscape of St. Francis, I discovered the face of St. Francis within me. As a pilgrim I had a destination: the real and mystical city of Assisi.

I had read lives of St. Francis from the time I was thirteen years old; in the Franciscan novitiate and in the college seminary, I studied Franciscan history and spirituality. I traveled from New Mexico to Ohio and back; but I'd never traveled abroad. Strangely, despite emotional exhaustion, neither destination (the outer or the inner) was unreasonably daunting because in the journeying I was experiencing, almost daily, spiritual awarenesses and a renewed creative energy. It was as if the very journey to Assisi was the muse for the voice of St. Francis within me.

From the moment I was pushed into my seat by the thrust of the jet engines lifting the Boeing 727 into the Cincinnati sky, I felt I was traveling not only to New York, and from there to Rome, but I was traveling back in time; middle-aged, I was entering the Middle Ages; I was entering a time of the renaissance of Christian spirituality.

There is something of time-travel in all pilgrimage, of course. We are usually going to a shrine or place where something spiritual happened in the past, an event that continues to radiate spirituality today. The way into that spiritual energy is the journey itself, made in prayer; with a repentant heart; with a sense of expiation for the right roads we didn't take, the false roads we walked instead; and with a desire to make up for something.

This expiation could be for personal sin, or for the collective sin of the world, or for the lack of faith we perceive in ourselves and others, and even to facilitate the entrance into heaven of our loved ones; in the case of a saint, even of one's enemies.

Because the pilgrimage is weighted with all the above spiritual valences, it is from the beginning an endeavor to touch the parallel and interior world of the Spirit. Because we are open to the world of the Spirit, we begin to experience a gradual transformation of the way we look at ourselves and at the world around us.

If we travel with others, we are very soon aware of how disparate are the people pilgrimage brings together: women and men, conservatives and liberals, saints and sinners, young and old, rich and poor, black and brown, yellow and white. The pilgrimage is a microcosm that in its progress gradually purifies, so that our own evils and prejudices are no longer projected onto the one who does not share our persuasions.

That the other is not to blame for all the world's ills slowly becomes clear. It is not the conservative or liberal, the religious or non-religious person who's to blame. Evil comes from every human heart, including one's own, as does virtue, if it is allowed to do so.

A transformation follows whereby we no longer blame but strive to redeem, to make holy, by allowing God's love and grace to inhabit us and then by sharing that love with others. This is the ultimate effect of pilgrimage. This is what the pilgrim strives for and walks toward. Pilgrimage opens our eyes to see the world with God's eyes, as far as humanly possible, and to experience the spiritual world that invites us to begin to pray and walk for those who are making the pilgrimage with us. We become a newborn pilgrim family.

Notes

PART ONE *The Pilgrim's Map*

p. 7 *"In the liturgy on earth . . . we appear with him in glory."*
The Liturgy of the Hours, III, Ordinary Time, Weeks 1–17 (New York: Catholic Publishing Co., 1975), 111-112.

p. 10 *"I deliberated with an aching heart . . . and the world lay spread before me."*
Charles Dickens. *Great Expectations* (Oxford: Oxford University Press, 1998), 151-152.

p. 11 *"Call me Ishmael . . . then I account it high time to get to seas as soon as I can.."*
Herman Melville, *Moby Dick, or The Whale* (New York: The Library of America, 1992), 795.

p. 12 *"The drama's done . . . only found another orphan"*
Melville, 1408.

p. 14 *"The pilgrim shall array himself . . . and a scrip."*
Jonathan Sumption, *Pilgrimage: An Image of Medieval Religion* (Totoway, NJ: Rowman and Littlefield, 1975), 171.

p. 15 *"He that be a pilgrim . . . and so go forth."*
Sumption, 168.

p. 15 *" . . . and a solemn ritual of initiation"*
Sumption, 168–171.

PART TWO *The Pilgrim's Credo*

p. 45 *"I advise, admonish, and exhort you . . . speaking honorably to everyone."*
Murray Bodo, *Through the Year with Francis of Assisi* (Cincinnati: St. Anthony Messenger Press, 1993), 88.

p. 47 *" . . . true virtue and salvation of soul."*
Dictated writing of St. Francis, translated by Bodo, *Through the Year with Francis of Assisi*, 152-153.

p. 57 *" . . . before I left the world."*
Translated by the author from Fonti Francescane, Editio Minor, (Assisi: Editrici Francescane, 1986), 66.

p. 60 *" . . . we have made little or no progress."*
1 Cel. 103, *St Francis of Assisi: Writings and Early Biographies.* ed. by Marion A. Habig (Chicago: Franciscan Herald Press, 1973), 318.

p. 66 *"Praise to you, my Lord . . . Humbly but grandly."*
Author's translation.

p. 71 *" . . . he will become a son of God."*
Habig, 891.

p. 91 *"We shall not cease from exploration . . . and know the place for the first time."*
T.S. Eliot, *The Complete Poems and Plays 1909–1950* (New York: Harcourt Brace and Co., 1980), 145.

PART THREE *Meditations on Returning Home*

p. 95 Lines from the poem "Morning" reprinted from the book *Circus Days and Nights* by Robert Lax, edited by Paul J. Spaeth, copyright © 2000 by Robert Lax. Reprinted with the permission of The Overlook Press.